C-771   CAREER EXAMINATION SERIES

This is your
PASSBOOK for...

Storekeeper

Test Preparation Study Guide
Questions & Answers

COPYRIGHT NOTICE

This book is SOLELY intended for, is sold ONLY to, and its use is RESTRICTED to individual, bona fide applicants or candidates who qualify by virtue of having seriously filed applications for appropriate license, certificate, professional and/or promotional advancement, higher school matriculation, scholarship, or other legitimate requirements of education and/or governmental authorities.

This book is NOT intended for use, class instruction, tutoring, training, duplication, copying, reprinting, excerption, or adaptation, etc., by:

1) Other publishers
2) Proprietors and/or Instructors of "Coaching" and/or Preparatory Courses
3) Personnel and/or Training Divisions of commercial, industrial, and governmental organizations
4) Schools, colleges, or universities and/or their departments and staffs, including teachers and other personnel
5) Testing Agencies or Bureaus
6) Study groups which seek by the purchase of a single volume to copy and/or duplicate and/or adapt this material for use by the group as a whole without having purchased individual volumes for each of the members of the group
7) Et al.

Such persons would be in violation of appropriate Federal and State statutes.

PROVISION OF LICENSING AGREEMENTS – Recognized educational, commercial, industrial, and governmental institutions and organizations, and others legitimately engaged in educational pursuits, including training, testing, and measurement activities, may address request for a licensing agreement to the copyright owners, who will determine whether, and under what conditions, including fees and charges, the materials in this book may be used them. In other words, a licensing facility exists for the legitimate use of the material in this book on other than an individual basis. However, it is asseverated and affirmed here that the material in this book CANNOT be used without the receipt of the express permission of such a licensing agreement from the Publishers. Inquiries re licensing should be addressed to the company, attention rights and permissions department.

All rights reserved, including the right of reproduction in whole or in part, in any form or by any means, electronic or mechanical, including photocopying, recording, or by any information storage and retrieval system, without permission in writing from the Publisher.

Copyright © 2025 by
National Learning Corporation

212 Michael Drive, Syosset, NY 11791
(516) 921-8888 • www.passbooks.com
E-mail: info@passbooks.com

PASSBOOK® SERIES

THE *PASSBOOK® SERIES* has been created to prepare applicants and candidates for the ultimate academic battlefield – the examination room.

At some time in our lives, each and every one of us may be required to take an examination – for validation, matriculation, admission, qualification, registration, certification, or licensure.

Based on the assumption that every applicant or candidate has met the basic formal educational standards, has taken the required number of courses, and read the necessary texts, the *PASSBOOK® SERIES* furnishes the one special preparation which may assure passing with confidence, instead of failing with insecurity. Examination questions – together with answers – are furnished as the basic vehicle for study so that the mysteries of the examination and its compounding difficulties may be eliminated or diminished by a sure method.

This book is meant to help you pass your examination provided that you qualify and are serious in your objective.

The entire field is reviewed through the huge store of content information which is succinctly presented through a provocative and challenging approach – the question-and-answer method.

A climate of success is established by furnishing the correct answers at the end of each test.

You soon learn to recognize types of questions, forms of questions, and patterns of questioning. You may even begin to anticipate expected outcomes.

You perceive that many questions are repeated or adapted so that you can gain acute insights, which may enable you to score many sure points.

You learn how to confront new questions, or types of questions, and to attack them confidently and work out the correct answers.

You note objectives and emphases, and recognize pitfalls and dangers, so that you may make positive educational adjustments.

Moreover, you are kept fully informed in relation to new concepts, methods, practices, and directions in the field.

You discover that you are actually taking the examination all the time: you are preparing for the examination by "taking" an examination, not by reading extraneous and/or supererogatory textbooks.

In short, this PASSBOOK®, used directedly, should be an important factor in helping you to pass your test.

STOREKEEPER

DUTIES AND RESPONSIBILITIES:
Under direction, supervises a major section of a storehouse, or a consolidated storeroom, or an equivalent storage unit, the stores division of a hospital, or perform field work; performs related work. The work involves responsibility for supervising the storeroom of a large department which includes responsibility for requisitioning, receiving, storing and distribution of a wide variety of supplies such as office supplies and furniture, automotive equipment and parts, gasoline, oil, tools, heavy equipment needed by department employees. An employee in this class is responsible for maintaining complete, accurate and up to date records of all transactions and maintaining security of the storeroom items. Does related work as required.

EXAMPLES OF TYPICAL TASKS:
Is responsible for the receipt, classification, storage, care, distribution, requisitioning, and inventory of materials, tools, supplies, and equipment. Supervises and assigns work to subordinate employees. Supervises the maintenance of perpetual inventories, checking uniformity and accuracy of postings. Prepares requisitions for stock replacement. Develops methods and procedures for handling and storing stock. Prepares lists of surplus, obsolete or obsolescent materials, and arranges for their transfer or other disposition. Takes necessary precautions to protect stock from deterioration or spoilage. Supervises loading, unloading, and dispatching of trucks. May, when necessary, load and unload at the storehouse and at the point of pick-up, delivery, or distribution. For this purpose, may travel to point of pick-up, delivery, or distribution. Also operates equipment necessary to perform loading and unloading. May prepare data for budget estimates necessary to perform loading and unloading. May prepare data for budget estimates for materials, tools, supplies, and equipment. Performs field work by visiting, inspecting, instructing, and advising stores personnel at various locations on the storage, distribution, and inventory control, etc., of materials, supplies, and equipment. Contacts vendors and discusses deliveries, shipments, amounts of shortage, etc. May act as principal assistant to a Senior Storekeeper. Keeps records and prepares reports.

SCOPE OF THE EXAMINATION:
The written test will be designed to test for knowledge, skills, and/or abilities as follows:
1. **Arithmetic computation with calculator** - These questions test for the ability to use a calculator to do basic computations. Questions will involve addition, subtraction, multiplication and division. You may also be asked to calculate averages, to use percents, and to round an answer to the nearest whole number.
2. **Keeping simple inventory records** - These questions test for the ability to follow instructions in keeping simple inventory records of different materials received and distributed from a central location. The ability to add, subtract, multiply, and divide will be required. You may have to compute total costs from quantities (number of units) and cost or price per unit. Knowledge of specific record keeping systems and techniques will not be needed.
3. **Principles and practices of storekeeping and inventory control** - These questions will test for candidates' knowledge of the principles guiding large scale storekeeping operations and their ability to put them into practice. Some of the areas covered may include analysis of rates of use, the determination of reorder points, choosing locations for the storage of goods, and determining how to handle stock to maximize the efficiency of the operation. Some arithmetic computation may be necessary.
4. **Supervision** - These questions test for knowledge of the principles and practices employed in planning, organizing, and controlling the activities of a work unit toward predetermined objectives. The concepts covered, usually in a situational question format, include such topics as assigning and reviewing work; evaluating performance; maintaining work standards; motivating and developing subordinates; implementing procedural change; increasing efficiency; and dealing with problems of absenteeism, morale, and discipline.

HOW TO TAKE A TEST

I. YOU MUST PASS AN EXAMINATION

A. WHAT EVERY CANDIDATE SHOULD KNOW

Examination applicants often ask us for help in preparing for the written test. What can I study in advance? What kinds of questions will be asked? How will the test be given? How will the papers be graded?

As an applicant for a civil service examination, you may be wondering about some of these things. Our purpose here is to suggest effective methods of advance study and to describe civil service examinations.

Your chances for success on this examination can be increased if you know how to prepare. Those "pre-examination jitters" can be reduced if you know what to expect. You can even experience an adventure in good citizenship if you know why civil service exams are given.

B. WHY ARE CIVIL SERVICE EXAMINATIONS GIVEN?

Civil service examinations are important to you in two ways. As a citizen, you want public jobs filled by employees who know how to do their work. As a job seeker, you want a fair chance to compete for that job on an equal footing with other candidates. The best-known means of accomplishing this two-fold goal is the competitive examination.

Exams are widely publicized throughout the nation. They may be administered for jobs in federal, state, city, municipal, town or village governments or agencies.

Any citizen may apply, with some limitations, such as the age or residence of applicants. Your experience and education may be reviewed to see whether you meet the requirements for the particular examination. When these requirements exist, they are reasonable and applied consistently to all applicants. Thus, a competitive examination may cause you some uneasiness now, but it is your privilege and safeguard.

C. HOW ARE CIVIL SERVICE EXAMS DEVELOPED?

Examinations are carefully written by trained technicians who are specialists in the field known as "psychological measurement," in consultation with recognized authorities in the field of work that the test will cover. These experts recommend the subject matter areas or skills to be tested; only those knowledges or skills important to your success on the job are included. The most reliable books and source materials available are used as references. Together, the experts and technicians judge the difficulty level of the questions.

Test technicians know how to phrase questions so that the problem is clearly stated. Their ethics do not permit "trick" or "catch" questions. Questions may have been tried out on sample groups, or subjected to statistical analysis, to determine their usefulness.

Written tests are often used in combination with performance tests, ratings of training and experience, and oral interviews. All of these measures combine to form the best-known means of finding the right person for the right job.

II. HOW TO PASS THE WRITTEN TEST

A. NATURE OF THE EXAMINATION

To prepare intelligently for civil service examinations, you should know how they differ from school examinations you have taken. In school you were assigned certain definite pages to read or subjects to cover. The examination questions were quite detailed and usually emphasized memory. Civil service exams, on the other hand, try to discover your present ability to perform the duties of a position, plus your potentiality to learn these duties. In other words, a civil service exam attempts to predict how successful you will be. Questions cover such a broad area that they cannot be as minute and detailed as school exam questions.

In the public service similar kinds of work, or positions, are grouped together in one "class." This process is known as *position-classification*. All the positions in a class are paid according to the salary range for that class. One class title covers all of these positions, and they are all tested by the same examination.

B. FOUR BASIC STEPS

1) Study the announcement

How, then, can you know what subjects to study? Our best answer is: "Learn as much as possible about the class of positions for which you've applied." The exam will test the knowledge, skills and abilities needed to do the work.

Your most valuable source of information about the position you want is the official exam announcement. This announcement lists the training and experience qualifications. Check these standards and apply only if you come reasonably close to meeting them.

The brief description of the position in the examination announcement offers some clues to the subjects which will be tested. Think about the job itself. Review the duties in your mind. Can you perform them, or are there some in which you are rusty? Fill in the blank spots in your preparation.

Many jurisdictions preview the written test in the exam announcement by including a section called "Knowledge and Abilities Required," "Scope of the Examination," or some similar heading. Here you will find out specifically what fields will be tested.

2) Review your own background

Once you learn in general what the position is all about, and what you need to know to do the work, ask yourself which subjects you already know fairly well and which need improvement. You may wonder whether to concentrate on improving your strong areas or on building some background in your fields of weakness. When the announcement has specified "some knowledge" or "considerable knowledge," or has used adjectives like "beginning principles of…" or "advanced … methods," you can get a clue as to the number and difficulty of questions to be asked in any given field. More questions, and hence broader coverage, would be included for those subjects which are more important in the work. Now weigh your strengths and weaknesses against the job requirements and prepare accordingly.

3) Determine the level of the position

Another way to tell how intensively you should prepare is to understand the level of the job for which you are applying. Is it the entering level? In other words, is this the position in which beginners in a field of work are hired? Or is it an intermediate or advanced level? Sometimes this is indicated by such words as "Junior" or "Senior" in the class title. Other jurisdictions use Roman numerals to designate the level – Clerk I, Clerk II, for example. The word "Supervisor" sometimes appears in the title. If the level is not indicated by the title, check the description of duties. Will you be working under very close supervision, or will you have responsibility for independent decisions in this work?

4) Choose appropriate study materials

Now that you know the subjects to be examined and the relative amount of each subject to be covered, you can choose suitable study materials. For beginning level jobs, or even advanced ones, if you have a pronounced weakness in some aspect of your training, read a modern, standard textbook in that field. Be sure it is up to date and has general coverage. Such books are normally available at your library, and the librarian will be glad to help you locate one. For entry-level positions, questions of appropriate difficulty are chosen – neither highly advanced questions, nor those too simple. Such questions require careful thought but not advanced training.

If the position for which you are applying is technical or advanced, you will read more advanced, specialized material. If you are already familiar with the basic principles of your field, elementary textbooks would waste your time. Concentrate on advanced textbooks and technical periodicals. Think through the concepts and review difficult problems in your field.

These are all general sources. You can get more ideas on your own initiative, following these leads. For example, training manuals and publications of the government agency which employs workers in your field can be useful, particularly for technical and professional positions. A letter or visit to the government department involved may result in more specific study suggestions, and certainly will provide you with a more definite idea of the exact nature of the position you are seeking.

III. KINDS OF TESTS

Tests are used for purposes other than measuring knowledge and ability to perform specified duties. For some positions, it is equally important to test ability to make adjustments to new situations or to profit from training. In others, basic mental abilities not dependent on information are essential. Questions which test these things may not appear as pertinent to the duties of the position as those which test for knowledge and information. Yet they are often highly important parts of a fair examination. For very general questions, it is almost impossible to help you direct your study efforts. What we can do is to point out some of the more common of these general abilities needed in public service positions and describe some typical questions.

1) General information

Broad, general information has been found useful for predicting job success in some kinds of work. This is tested in a variety of ways, from vocabulary lists to questions about current events. Basic background in some field of work, such as sociology or economics, may be sampled in a group of questions. Often these are principles which have become familiar to most persons through exposure rather than through formal training. It is difficult to advise you how to study for these questions; being alert to the world around you is our best suggestion.

2) Verbal ability

An example of an ability needed in many positions is verbal or language ability. Verbal ability is, in brief, the ability to use and understand words. Vocabulary and grammar tests are typical measures of this ability. Reading comprehension or paragraph interpretation questions are common in many kinds of civil service tests. You are given a paragraph of written material and asked to find its central meaning.

3) Numerical ability

Number skills can be tested by the familiar arithmetic problem, by checking paired lists of numbers to see which are alike and which are different, or by interpreting charts and graphs. In the latter test, a graph may be printed in the test booklet which you are asked to use as the basis for answering questions.

4) Observation

A popular test for law-enforcement positions is the observation test. A picture is shown to you for several minutes, then taken away. Questions about the picture test your ability to observe both details and larger elements.

5) Following directions

In many positions in the public service, the employee must be able to carry out written instructions dependably and accurately. You may be given a chart with several columns, each column listing a variety of information. The questions require you to carry out directions involving the information given in the chart.

6) Skills and aptitudes

Performance tests effectively measure some manual skills and aptitudes. When the skill is one in which you are trained, such as typing or shorthand, you can practice. These tests are often very much like those given in business school or high school courses. For many of the other skills and aptitudes, however, no short-time preparation can be made. Skills and abilities natural to you or that you have developed throughout your lifetime are being tested.

Many of the general questions just described provide all the data needed to answer the questions and ask you to use your reasoning ability to find the answers. Your best preparation for these tests, as well as for tests of facts and ideas, is to be at your physical and mental best. You, no doubt, have your own methods of getting into an exam-taking mood and keeping "in shape." The next section lists some ideas on this subject.

IV. KINDS OF QUESTIONS

Only rarely is the "essay" question, which you answer in narrative form, used in civil service tests. Civil service tests are usually of the short-answer type. Full instructions for answering these questions will be given to you at the examination. But in case this is your first experience with short-answer questions and separate answer sheets, here is what you need to know:

1) Multiple-choice Questions

Most popular of the short-answer questions is the "multiple choice" or "best answer" question. It can be used, for example, to test for factual knowledge, ability to solve problems or judgment in meeting situations found at work.

A multiple-choice question is normally one of three types—
- It can begin with an incomplete statement followed by several possible endings. You are to find the one ending which *best* completes the statement, although some of the others may not be entirely wrong.
- It can also be a complete statement in the form of a question which is answered by choosing one of the statements listed.

- It can be in the form of a problem – again you select the best answer.

Here is an example of a multiple-choice question with a discussion which should give you some clues as to the method for choosing the right answer:

When an employee has a complaint about his assignment, the action which will *best* help him overcome his difficulty is to
   A. discuss his difficulty with his coworkers
   B. take the problem to the head of the organization
   C. take the problem to the person who gave him the assignment
   D. say nothing to anyone about his complaint

In answering this question, you should study each of the choices to find which is best. Consider choice "A" – Certainly an employee may discuss his complaint with fellow employees, but no change or improvement can result, and the complaint remains unresolved. Choice "B" is a poor choice since the head of the organization probably does not know what assignment you have been given, and taking your problem to him is known as "going over the head" of the supervisor. The supervisor, or person who made the assignment, is the person who can clarify it or correct any injustice. Choice "C" is, therefore, correct. To say nothing, as in choice "D," is unwise. Supervisors have and interest in knowing the problems employees are facing, and the employee is seeking a solution to his problem.

2) True/False Questions

The "true/false" or "right/wrong" form of question is sometimes used. Here a complete statement is given. Your job is to decide whether the statement is right or wrong.

SAMPLE: A roaming cell-phone call to a nearby city costs less than a non-roaming call to a distant city.

This statement is wrong, or false, since roaming calls are more expensive.

This is not a complete list of all possible question forms, although most of the others are variations of these common types. You will always get complete directions for answering questions. Be sure you understand *how* to mark your answers – ask questions until you do.

V. RECORDING YOUR ANSWERS

Computer terminals are used more and more today for many different kinds of exams.
For an examination with very few applicants, you may be told to record your answers in the test booklet itself. Separate answer sheets are much more common. If this separate answer sheet is to be scored by machine – and this is often the case – it is highly important that you mark your answers correctly in order to get credit.

An electronic scoring machine is often used in civil service offices because of the speed with which papers can be scored. Machine-scored answer sheets must be marked with a pencil, which will be given to you. This pencil has a high graphite content which responds to the electronic scoring machine. As a matter of fact, stray dots may register as answers, so do not let your pencil rest on the answer sheet while you are pondering the correct answer. Also, if your pencil lead breaks or is otherwise defective, ask for another.

Since the answer sheet will be dropped in a slot in the scoring machine, be careful not to bend the corners or get the paper crumpled.

The answer sheet normally has five vertical columns of numbers, with 30 numbers to a column. These numbers correspond to the question numbers in your test booklet. After each number, going across the page are four or five pairs of dotted lines. These short dotted lines have small letters or numbers above them. The first two pairs may also have a "T" or "F" above the letters. This indicates that the first two pairs only are to be used if the questions are of the true-false type. If the questions are multiple choice, disregard the "T" and "F" and pay attention only to the small letters or numbers.

Answer your questions in the manner of the sample that follows:

32. The largest city in the United States is
    A. Washington, D.C.
    B. New York City
    C. Chicago
    D. Detroit
    E. San Francisco

1) Choose the answer you think is best. (New York City is the largest, so "B" is correct.)
2) Find the row of dotted lines numbered the same as the question you are answering. (Find row number 32)
3) Find the pair of dotted lines corresponding to the answer. (Find the pair of lines under the mark "B.")
4) Make a solid black mark between the dotted lines.

VI. BEFORE THE TEST

Common sense will help you find procedures to follow to get ready for an examination. Too many of us, however, overlook these sensible measures. Indeed, nervousness and fatigue have been found to be the most serious reasons why applicants fail to do their best on civil service tests. Here is a list of reminders:

- Begin your preparation early – Don't wait until the last minute to go scurrying around for books and materials or to find out what the position is all about.
- Prepare continuously – An hour a night for a week is better than an all-night cram session. This has been definitely established. What is more, a night a week for a month will return better dividends than crowding your study into a shorter period of time.
- Locate the place of the exam – You have been sent a notice telling you when and where to report for the examination. If the location is in a different town or otherwise unfamiliar to you, it would be well to inquire the best route and learn something about the building.
- Relax the night before the test – Allow your mind to rest. Do not study at all that night. Plan some mild recreation or diversion; then go to bed early and get a good night's sleep.
- Get up early enough to make a leisurely trip to the place for the test – This way unforeseen events, traffic snarls, unfamiliar buildings, etc. will not upset you.
- Dress comfortably – A written test is not a fashion show. You will be known by number and not by name, so wear something comfortable.

- Leave excess paraphernalia at home – Shopping bags and odd bundles will get in your way. You need bring only the items mentioned in the official notice you received; usually everything you need is provided. Do not bring reference books to the exam. They will only confuse those last minutes and be taken away from you when in the test room.
- Arrive somewhat ahead of time – If because of transportation schedules you must get there very early, bring a newspaper or magazine to take your mind off yourself while waiting.
- Locate the examination room – When you have found the proper room, you will be directed to the seat or part of the room where you will sit. Sometimes you are given a sheet of instructions to read while you are waiting. Do not fill out any forms until you are told to do so; just read them and be prepared.
- Relax and prepare to listen to the instructions
- If you have any physical problem that may keep you from doing your best, be sure to tell the test administrator. If you are sick or in poor health, you really cannot do your best on the exam. You can come back and take the test some other time.

VII. AT THE TEST

The day of the test is here and you have the test booklet in your hand. The temptation to get going is very strong. Caution! There is more to success than knowing the right answers. You must know how to identify your papers and understand variations in the type of short-answer question used in this particular examination. Follow these suggestions for maximum results from your efforts:

1) Cooperate with the monitor

The test administrator has a duty to create a situation in which you can be as much at ease as possible. He will give instructions, tell you when to begin, check to see that you are marking your answer sheet correctly, and so on. He is not there to guard you, although he will see that your competitors do not take unfair advantage. He wants to help you do your best.

2) Listen to all instructions

Don't jump the gun! Wait until you understand all directions. In most civil service tests you get more time than you need to answer the questions. So don't be in a hurry. Read each word of instructions until you clearly understand the meaning. Study the examples, listen to all announcements and follow directions. Ask questions if you do not understand what to do.

3) Identify your papers

Civil service exams are usually identified by number only. You will be assigned a number; you must not put your name on your test papers. Be sure to copy your number correctly. Since more than one exam may be given, copy your exact examination title.

4) Plan your time

Unless you are told that a test is a "speed" or "rate of work" test, speed itself is usually not important. Time enough to answer all the questions will be provided, but this does not mean that you have all day. An overall time limit has been set. Divide the total time (in minutes) by the number of questions to determine the approximate time you have for each question.

5) Do not linger over difficult questions

If you come across a difficult question, mark it with a paper clip (useful to have along) and come back to it when you have been through the booklet. One caution if you do this – be sure to skip a number on your answer sheet as well. Check often to be sure that you have not lost your place and that you are marking in the row numbered the same as the question you are answering.

6) Read the questions

Be sure you know what the question asks! Many capable people are unsuccessful because they failed to *read* the questions correctly.

7) Answer all questions

Unless you have been instructed that a penalty will be deducted for incorrect answers, it is better to guess than to omit a question.

8) Speed tests

It is often better NOT to guess on speed tests. It has been found that on timed tests people are tempted to spend the last few seconds before time is called in marking answers at random – without even reading them – in the hope of picking up a few extra points. To discourage this practice, the instructions may warn you that your score will be "corrected" for guessing. That is, a penalty will be applied. The incorrect answers will be deducted from the correct ones, or some other penalty formula will be used.

9) Review your answers

If you finish before time is called, go back to the questions you guessed or omitted to give them further thought. Review other answers if you have time.

10) Return your test materials

If you are ready to leave before others have finished or time is called, take ALL your materials to the monitor and leave quietly. Never take any test material with you. The monitor can discover whose papers are not complete, and taking a test booklet may be grounds for disqualification.

VIII. EXAMINATION TECHNIQUES

1) Read the general instructions carefully. These are usually printed on the first page of the exam booklet. As a rule, these instructions refer to the timing of the examination; the fact that you should not start work until the signal and must stop work at a signal, etc. If there are any *special* instructions, such as a choice of questions to be answered, make sure that you note this instruction carefully.

2) When you are ready to start work on the examination, that is as soon as the signal has been given, read the instructions to each question booklet, underline any key words or phrases, such as *least, best, outline, describe* and the like. In this way you will tend to answer as requested rather than discover on reviewing your paper that you *listed without describing*, that you selected the *worst* choice rather than the *best* choice, etc.

3) If the examination is of the objective or multiple-choice type – that is, each question will also give a series of possible answers: A, B, C or D, and you are called upon to select the best answer and write the letter next to that answer on your answer paper – it is advisable to start answering each question in turn. There may be anywhere from 50 to 100 such questions in the three or four hours allotted and you can see how much time would be taken if you read through all the questions before beginning to answer any. Furthermore, if you come across a question or group of questions which you know would be difficult to answer, it would undoubtedly affect your handling of all the other questions.

4) If the examination is of the essay type and contains but a few questions, it is a moot point as to whether you should read all the questions before starting to answer any one. Of course, if you are given a choice – say five out of seven and the like – then it is essential to read all the questions so you can eliminate the two that are most difficult. If, however, you are asked to answer all the questions, there may be danger in trying to answer the easiest one first because you may find that you will spend too much time on it. The best technique is to answer the first question, then proceed to the second, etc.

5) Time your answers. Before the exam begins, write down the time it started, then add the time allowed for the examination and write down the time it must be completed, then divide the time available somewhat as follows:
    - If 3-1/2 hours are allowed, that would be 210 minutes. If you have 80 objective-type questions, that would be an average of 2-1/2 minutes per question. Allow yourself no more than 2 minutes per question, or a total of 160 minutes, which will permit about 50 minutes to review.
    - If for the time allotment of 210 minutes there are 7 essay questions to answer, that would average about 30 minutes a question. Give yourself only 25 minutes per question so that you have about 35 minutes to review.

6) The most important instruction is to *read each question* and make sure you know what is wanted. The second most important instruction is to *time yourself properly* so that you answer every question. The third most important instruction is to *answer every question*. Guess if you have to but include something for each question. Remember that you will receive no credit for a blank and will probably receive some credit if you write something in answer to an essay question. If you guess a letter – say "B" for a multiple-choice question – you may have guessed right. If you leave a blank as an answer to a multiple-choice question, the examiners may respect your feelings but it will not add a point to your score. Some exams may penalize you for wrong answers, so in such cases *only*, you may not want to guess unless you have some basis for your answer.

7) Suggestions
    a. Objective-type questions
        1. Examine the question booklet for proper sequence of pages and questions
        2. Read all instructions carefully
        3. Skip any question which seems too difficult; return to it after all other questions have been answered
        4. Apportion your time properly; do not spend too much time on any single question or group of questions

5. Note and underline key words – *all, most, fewest, least, best, worst, same, opposite,* etc.
6. Pay particular attention to negatives
7. Note unusual option, e.g., unduly long, short, complex, different or similar in content to the body of the question
8. Observe the use of "hedging" words – *probably, may, most likely,* etc.
9. Make sure that your answer is put next to the same number as the question
10. Do not second-guess unless you have good reason to believe the second answer is definitely more correct
11. Cross out original answer if you decide another answer is more accurate; do not erase until you are ready to hand your paper in
12. Answer all questions; guess unless instructed otherwise
13. Leave time for review

   b. Essay questions
1. Read each question carefully
2. Determine exactly what is wanted. Underline key words or phrases.
3. Decide on outline or paragraph answer
4. Include many different points and elements unless asked to develop any one or two points or elements
5. Show impartiality by giving pros and cons unless directed to select one side only
6. Make and write down any assumptions you find necessary to answer the questions
7. Watch your English, grammar, punctuation and choice of words
8. Time your answers; don't crowd material

8) Answering the essay question

Most essay questions can be answered by framing the specific response around several key words or ideas. Here are a few such key words or ideas:

M's: manpower, materials, methods, money, management
P's: purpose, program, policy, plan, procedure, practice, problems, pitfalls, personnel, public relations

   a. Six basic steps in handling problems:
1. Preliminary plan and background development
2. Collect information, data and facts
3. Analyze and interpret information, data and facts
4. Analyze and develop solutions as well as make recommendations
5. Prepare report and sell recommendations
6. Install recommendations and follow up effectiveness

   b. Pitfalls to avoid
1. *Taking things for granted* – A statement of the situation does not necessarily imply that each of the elements is necessarily true; for example, a complaint may be invalid and biased so that all that can be taken for granted is that a complaint has been registered

2. *Considering only one side of a situation* – Wherever possible, indicate several alternatives and then point out the reasons you selected the best one
3. *Failing to indicate follow up* – Whenever your answer indicates action on your part, make certain that you will take proper follow-up action to see how successful your recommendations, procedures or actions turn out to be
4. *Taking too long in answering any single question* – Remember to time your answers properly

IX. AFTER THE TEST

Scoring procedures differ in detail among civil service jurisdictions although the general principles are the same. Whether the papers are hand-scored or graded by machine we have described, they are nearly always graded by number. That is, the person who marks the paper knows only the number – never the name – of the applicant. Not until all the papers have been graded will they be matched with names. If other tests, such as training and experience or oral interview ratings have been given, scores will be combined. Different parts of the examination usually have different weights. For example, the written test might count 60 percent of the final grade, and a rating of training and experience 40 percent. In many jurisdictions, veterans will have a certain number of points added to their grades.

After the final grade has been determined, the names are placed in grade order and an eligible list is established. There are various methods for resolving ties between those who get the same final grade – probably the most common is to place first the name of the person whose application was received first. Job offers are made from the eligible list in the order the names appear on it. You will be notified of your grade and your rank as soon as all these computations have been made. This will be done as rapidly as possible.

People who are found to meet the requirements in the announcement are called "eligibles." Their names are put on a list of eligible candidates. An eligible's chances of getting a job depend on how high he stands on this list and how fast agencies are filling jobs from the list.

When a job is to be filled from a list of eligibles, the agency asks for the names of people on the list of eligibles for that job. When the civil service commission receives this request, it sends to the agency the names of the three people highest on this list. Or, if the job to be filled has specialized requirements, the office sends the agency the names of the top three persons who meet these requirements from the general list.

The appointing officer makes a choice from among the three people whose names were sent to him. If the selected person accepts the appointment, the names of the others are put back on the list to be considered for future openings.

That is the rule in hiring from all kinds of eligible lists, whether they are for typist, carpenter, chemist, or something else. For every vacancy, the appointing officer has his choice of any one of the top three eligibles on the list. This explains why the person whose name is on top of the list sometimes does not get an appointment when some of the persons lower on the list do. If the appointing officer chooses the second or third eligible, the No. 1 eligible does not get a job at once, but stays on the list until he is appointed or the list is terminated.

X. HOW TO PASS THE INTERVIEW TEST

The examination for which you applied requires an oral interview test. You have already taken the written test and you are now being called for the interview test – the final part of the formal examination.

You may think that it is not possible to prepare for an interview test and that there are no procedures to follow during an interview. Our purpose is to point out some things you can do in advance that will help you and some good rules to follow and pitfalls to avoid while you are being interviewed.

What is an interview supposed to test?

The written examination is designed to test the technical knowledge and competence of the candidate; the oral is designed to evaluate intangible qualities, not readily measured otherwise, and to establish a list showing the relative fitness of each candidate – as measured against his competitors – for the position sought. Scoring is not on the basis of "right" and "wrong," but on a sliding scale of values ranging from "not passable" to "outstanding." As a matter of fact, it is possible to achieve a relatively low score without a single "incorrect" answer because of evident weakness in the qualities being measured.

Occasionally, an examination may consist entirely of an oral test – either an individual or a group oral. In such cases, information is sought concerning the technical knowledges and abilities of the candidate, since there has been no written examination for this purpose. More commonly, however, an oral test is used to supplement a written examination.

Who conducts interviews?

The composition of oral boards varies among different jurisdictions. In nearly all, a representative of the personnel department serves as chairman. One of the members of the board may be a representative of the department in which the candidate would work. In some cases, "outside experts" are used, and, frequently, a businessman or some other representative of the general public is asked to serve. Labor and management or other special groups may be represented. The aim is to secure the services of experts in the appropriate field.

However the board is composed, it is a good idea (and not at all improper or unethical) to ascertain in advance of the interview who the members are and what groups they represent. When you are introduced to them, you will have some idea of their backgrounds and interests, and at least you will not stutter and stammer over their names.

What should be done before the interview?

While knowledge about the board members is useful and takes some of the surprise element out of the interview, there is other preparation which is more substantive. It *is* possible to prepare for an oral interview – in several ways:

1) Keep a copy of your application and review it carefully before the interview

This may be the only document before the oral board, and the starting point of the interview. Know what education and experience you have listed there, and the sequence and dates of all of it. Sometimes the board will ask you to review the highlights of your experience for them; you should not have to hem and haw doing it.

2) Study the class specification and the examination announcement

Usually, the oral board has one or both of these to guide them. The qualities, characteristics or knowledges required by the position sought are stated in these documents. They offer valuable clues as to the nature of the oral interview. For example, if the job involves supervisory responsibilities, the announcement will usually indicate that knowledge of modern supervisory methods and the qualifications of the candidate as a supervisor will be tested. If so, you can expect such questions, frequently in the form of a hypothetical situation which you are expected to solve. NEVER go into an oral without knowledge of the duties and responsibilities of the job you seek.

3) Think through each qualification required

Try to visualize the kind of questions you would ask if you were a board member. How well could you answer them? Try especially to appraise your own knowledge and background in each area, *measured against the job sought*, and identify any areas in which you are weak. Be critical and realistic – do not flatter yourself.

4) Do some general reading in areas in which you feel you may be weak

For example, if the job involves supervision and your past experience has NOT, some general reading in supervisory methods and practices, particularly in the field of human relations, might be useful. Do NOT study agency procedures or detailed manuals. The oral board will be testing your understanding and capacity, not your memory.

5) Get a good night's sleep and watch your general health and mental attitude

You will want a clear head at the interview. Take care of a cold or any other minor ailment, and of course, no hangovers.

What should be done on the day of the interview?

Now comes the day of the interview itself. Give yourself plenty of time to get there. Plan to arrive somewhat ahead of the scheduled time, particularly if your appointment is in the fore part of the day. If a previous candidate fails to appear, the board might be ready for you a bit early. By early afternoon an oral board is almost invariably behind schedule if there are many candidates, and you may have to wait. Take along a book or magazine to read, or your application to review, but leave any extraneous material in the waiting room when you go in for your interview. In any event, relax and compose yourself.

The matter of dress is important. The board is forming impressions about you – from your experience, your manners, your attitude, and your appearance. Give your personal appearance careful attention. Dress your best, but not your flashiest. Choose conservative, appropriate clothing, and be sure it is immaculate. This is a business interview, and your appearance should indicate that you regard it as such. Besides, being well groomed and properly dressed will help boost your confidence.

Sooner or later, someone will call your name and escort you into the interview room. *This is it.* From here on you are on your own. It is too late for any more preparation. But remember, you asked for this opportunity to prove your fitness, and you are here because your request was granted.

What happens when you go in?

The usual sequence of events will be as follows: The clerk (who is often the board stenographer) will introduce you to the chairman of the oral board, who will introduce you to the other members of the board. Acknowledge the introductions before you sit down. Do not be surprised if you find a microphone facing you or a stenotypist sitting by. Oral interviews are usually recorded in the event of an appeal or other review.

Usually the chairman of the board will open the interview by reviewing the highlights of your education and work experience from your application – primarily for the benefit of the other members of the board, as well as to get the material into the record. Do not interrupt or comment unless there is an error or significant misinterpretation; if that is the case, do not hesitate. But do not quibble about insignificant matters. Also, he will usually ask you some question about your education, experience or your present job – partly to get you to start talking and to establish the interviewing "rapport." He may start the actual questioning, or turn it over to one of the other members. Frequently, each member undertakes the questioning on a particular area, one in which he is perhaps most competent, so you can expect each member to participate in the examination. Because time is limited, you may also expect some rather abrupt switches in the direction the questioning takes, so do not be upset by it. Normally, a board member will not pursue a single line of questioning unless he discovers a particular strength or weakness.

After each member has participated, the chairman will usually ask whether any member has any further questions, then will ask you if you have anything you wish to add. Unless you are expecting this question, it may floor you. Worse, it may start you off on an extended, extemporaneous speech. The board is not usually seeking more information. The question is principally to offer you a last opportunity to present further qualifications or to indicate that you have nothing to add. So, if you feel that a significant qualification or characteristic has been overlooked, it is proper to point it out in a sentence or so. Do not compliment the board on the thoroughness of their examination – they have been sketchy, and you know it. If you wish, merely say, "No thank you, I have nothing further to add." This is a point where you can "talk yourself out" of a good impression or fail to present an important bit of information. Remember, *you close the interview yourself*.

The chairman will then say, "That is all, Mr. _____, thank you." Do not be startled; the interview is over, and quicker than you think. Thank him, gather your belongings and take your leave. Save your sigh of relief for the other side of the door.

How to put your best foot forward

Throughout this entire process, you may feel that the board individually and collectively is trying to pierce your defenses, seek out your hidden weaknesses and embarrass and confuse you. Actually, this is not true. They are obliged to make an appraisal of your qualifications for the job you are seeking, and they want to see you in your best light. Remember, they must interview all candidates and a non-cooperative candidate may become a failure in spite of their best efforts to bring out his qualifications. Here are 15 suggestions that will help you:

1) **Be natural – Keep your attitude confident, not cocky**

If you are not confident that you can do the job, do not expect the board to be. Do not apologize for your weaknesses, try to bring out your strong points. The board is interested in a positive, not negative, presentation. Cockiness will antagonize any board member and make him wonder if you are covering up a weakness by a false show of strength.

2) **Get comfortable, but don't lounge or sprawl**

Sit erectly but not stiffly. A careless posture may lead the board to conclude that you are careless in other things, or at least that you are not impressed by the importance of the occasion. Either conclusion is natural, even if incorrect. Do not fuss with your clothing, a pencil or an ashtray. Your hands may occasionally be useful to emphasize a point; do not let them become a point of distraction.

3) **Do not wisecrack or make small talk**

This is a serious situation, and your attitude should show that you consider it as such. Further, the time of the board is limited – they do not want to waste it, and neither should you.

4) Do not exaggerate your experience or abilities

In the first place, from information in the application or other interviews and sources, the board may know more about you than you think. Secondly, you probably will not get away with it. An experienced board is rather adept at spotting such a situation, so do not take the chance.

5) If you know a board member, do not make a point of it, yet do not hide it

Certainly you are not fooling him, and probably not the other members of the board. Do not try to take advantage of your acquaintanceship – it will probably do you little good.

6) Do not dominate the interview

Let the board do that. They will give you the clues – do not assume that you have to do all the talking. Realize that the board has a number of questions to ask you, and do not try to take up all the interview time by showing off your extensive knowledge of the answer to the first one.

7) Be attentive

You only have 20 minutes or so, and you should keep your attention at its sharpest throughout. When a member is addressing a problem or question to you, give him your undivided attention. Address your reply principally to him, but do not exclude the other board members.

8) Do not interrupt

A board member may be stating a problem for you to analyze. He will ask you a question when the time comes. Let him state the problem, and wait for the question.

9) Make sure you understand the question

Do not try to answer until you are sure what the question is. If it is not clear, restate it in your own words or ask the board member to clarify it for you. However, do not haggle about minor elements.

10) Reply promptly but not hastily

A common entry on oral board rating sheets is "candidate responded readily," or "candidate hesitated in replies." Respond as promptly and quickly as you can, but do not jump to a hasty, ill-considered answer.

11) Do not be peremptory in your answers

A brief answer is proper – but do not fire your answer back. That is a losing game from your point of view. The board member can probably ask questions much faster than you can answer them.

12) Do not try to create the answer you think the board member wants

He is interested in what kind of mind you have and how it works – not in playing games. Furthermore, he can usually spot this practice and will actually grade you down on it.

13) Do not switch sides in your reply merely to agree with a board member

Frequently, a member will take a contrary position merely to draw you out and to see if you are willing and able to defend your point of view. Do not start a debate, yet do not surrender a good position. If a position is worth taking, it is worth defending.

14) Do not be afraid to admit an error in judgment if you are shown to be wrong

The board knows that you are forced to reply without any opportunity for careful consideration. Your answer may be demonstrably wrong. If so, admit it and get on with the interview.

15) Do not dwell at length on your present job

The opening question may relate to your present assignment. Answer the question but do not go into an extended discussion. You are being examined for a *new* job, not your present one. As a matter of fact, try to phrase ALL your answers in terms of the job for which you are being examined.

Basis of Rating

Probably you will forget most of these "do's" and "don'ts" when you walk into the oral interview room. Even remembering them all will not ensure you a passing grade. Perhaps you did not have the qualifications in the first place. But remembering them will help you to put your best foot forward, without treading on the toes of the board members.

Rumor and popular opinion to the contrary notwithstanding, an oral board wants you to make the best appearance possible. They know you are under pressure – but they also want to see how you respond to it as a guide to what your reaction would be under the pressures of the job you seek. They will be influenced by the degree of poise you display, the personal traits you show and the manner in which you respond.

ABOUT THIS BOOK

This book contains tests divided into Examination Sections. Go through each test, answering every question in the margin. We have also attached a sample answer sheet at the back of the book that can be removed and used. At the end of each test look at the answer key and check your answers. On the ones you got wrong, look at the right answer choice and learn. Do not fill in the answers first. Do not memorize the questions and answers, but understand the answer and principles involved. On your test, the questions will likely be different from the samples. Questions are changed and new ones added. If you understand these past questions you should have success with any changes that arise. Tests may consist of several types of questions. We have additional books on each subject should more study be advisable or necessary for you. Finally, the more you study, the better prepared you will be. This book is intended to be the last thing you study before you walk into the examination room. Prior study of relevant texts is also recommended. NLC publishes some of these in our Fundamental Series. Knowledge and good sense are important factors in passing your exam. Good luck also helps. So now study this Passbook, absorb the material contained within and take that knowledge into the examination. Then do your best to pass that exam.

EXAMINATION SECTION

EXAMINATION SECTION
TEST 1

DIRECTIONS: Each question or incomplete statement is followed by several suggested answers or completions. Select the one that BEST answers the question or completes the statement. *PRINT THE LETTER OF THE CORRECT ANSWER IN THE SPACE AT THE RIGHT.*

1. Of the following, the MOST probable hazard in storing subsistence supplies, such as meats and cereal products, is

    A. breakage
    B. flammability
    C. spillage
    D. spoilage

2. Of the following, the one which is usually LEAST likely to be shown on properly maintained bin tags is the

    A. amount received
    B. amount withdrawn
    C. anticipated yearly need
    D. balance on hand

3. Use of materials handling equipment rather than man-power for handling heavy loads generally results in

    A. increased danger of back injuries
    B. increased productivity
    C. reduction of the height of piled materials
    D. reduced productivity

4. When reviewing the operations of a storage facility, of the following, it is LEAST important that the storekeeper review the

    A. safety standards being followed
    B. utilization of space for storage
    C. accuracy of storage records
    D. prices used in the preparation of purchase orders

5. A storekeeper in charge of a storehouse has a practice of issuing to only one or two employees the key to the security room where small items of very high dollar value are stored.
   This practice is generally

    A. *desirable;* it prevents items of small value from being placed in the security room
    B. *desirable;* it helps to fix responsibility for safeguarding the items in the security room
    C. *undesirable;* not even the storekeeper in charge should have a key to the security room of a storehouse
    D. *undesirable;* each employee of the storehouse should have a key to the security room

6. A basic reason for assigning commodity code numbers to purchased and stored items is to

    A. prevent pilferage
    B. increase the use of mechanized equipment

C. facilitate ready reference in communications
D. decrease flexibility of storage areas

7. Of the following, a well-managed storage operation is MOST likely to reduce the

   A. coordination between purchasing and stores operations
   B. idle time of operating personnel awaiting material
   C. turnover of stored materials
   D. utilization of mechanical aids

8. Which of the following is NOT an important reason for authorizing a purchasing department to control stores?

   A. Coordination of purchasing and stores may result in economies.
   B. Record keeping of materials in storage is closely associated with the purchase of materials.
   C. The storage division can inform purchasing of turnover of items to prevent overstocking or understocking.
   D. The storerooms will be near the points of use, reducing transportation costs.

9. Of the following, the MOST important daily maintenance requirement for electric forklift trucks is usually

   A. charging the batteries
   B. checking tire pressure
   C. greasing all fittings
   D. tightening the chain link belt of the lift

10. Generally, it is considered desirable practice to maintain stock at a three-months level of supply.
    Under what circumstances would it be MOST desirable to reduce stock levels to a one-month period?

    A. Discounts when buying larger quantities
    B. Few obsolete items
    C. Rapid deterioration of items
    D. Rising prices

11. The BEST pallet to use for transporting pallet unit loads in motor freight trucks and railroad cars is generally the _____ pallet.

    A. standard skid   B. straddle truck type
    C. 4-way entry   D. 2-way entry

12. You find that delivery of a certain item cannot possibly be made to a using agency by the date the using agency requested.
    Of the following, the MOST advisable course of action for you to take FIRST is to

    A. cancel the order and inform the using agency
    B. discuss the problem with the using agency
    C. notify the using agency to obtain the item through direct purchase
    D. schedule the delivery for the earliest possible date

13. In storing items such as batteries, twine, wire, baled textiles, and other commodities subject to damage or compression by weight, the MOST efficient means of storage is by use of 13.____

    A. bin type storage racks
    B. metal containers
    C. pallet adapters
    D. pinwheel stacks

14. Where a lateral haul of 600 feet is required to transport large quantities of pipe stock, the BEST equipment to use is a 14.____

    A. forklift truck
    B. gravity-roller conveyor
    C. stock selector truck
    D. tractor and trailers

15. One hundred cartons of paper towels are to be unloaded from a truck to the receiving platform. The floor of the truck is three feet above the platform.
    Of the following, the one that is MOST suitable to use for this purpose is a 15.____

    A. forklift truck
    B. four-wheel platform handtruck
    C. gravity conveyor
    D. hand-operated electric skid truck

16. The BEST of the following reasons for developing understudies to storehouse supervisory staff is that this practice 16.____

    A. assures that capable staff will not leave their jobs since they are certain to be promoted
    B. helps to assure continued efficiency in a storehouse when persons in important positions leave their jobs
    C. improves morale by demonstrating to employees the opportunities for advancement
    D. provides an opportunity for giving on-the-job training

17. It is said that the morale of a staff is usually a good indication of the quality of leadership exercised by the supervisor of the staff.
    Of the following, the BEST indication of high morale among a staff is: 17.____

    A. Disciplinary actions against members of the staff are rare
    B. It is seldom necessary for the staff to work overtime
    C. The staff is seldom late in reporting for work
    D. The staff subordinates personal desires in favor of group objectives

18. The primary responsibility of a supervisor is to 18.____

    A. gain the confidence and make friends of all his subordinates
    B. get the work done properly
    C. satisfy his superior and gain his respect
    D. train the men in new methods for doing the work

19. Of the following, the MOST important value of a manual of procedures is that it usually   19._____

    A. eliminates the need for on-the-job training
    B. decreases the span of control which can be exercised by individual supervisory personnel
    C. outlines methods of operation for ready reference
    D. provides concrete examples of work previously performed by employees

20. Reprimanding a subordinate when he has done something wrong should be done primarily in order to   20._____

    A. deter others from similar acts
    B. improve the subordinate's future performance
    C. maintain discipline
    D. uphold departmental rules

21. Assume that one of the three units in a storehouse under your supervision has developed a considerable backlog of unfilled orders, whereas the other two are up-to-date. The one of the following measures which it would usually be MOST desirable to take in order to reduce this backlog immediately is to   21._____

    A. do a study to increase the efficiency of the unit with the backlog of unfilled orders
    B. establish a deadline by which date the unit with the backlog of unfilled orders must complete all of its work
    C. establish an ordered overtime work schedule for the unit with the backlog of unfilled orders
    D. reassign on a temporary basis some workers from the other two units to the unit with the backlog of unfilled orders

22. The success of a program for training employees for current job competence may normally be measured BEST by the   22._____

    A. amount of enthusiasm displayed by the participants during the program
    B. extent to which the course content is used in daily operations
    C. length of time that the subject matter of the program is retained
    D. speed with which the subject matter of the program is learned

23. Of the following, the primary consideration in determining the number of people which one individual can supervise is the   23._____

    A. amount of time the individual can devote to supervision
    B. individual's knowledge of the work performed by the persons being supervised
    C. nature and variety of activities performed by the persons being supervised
    D. place where the work is performed

24. Assume that you, a storekeeper in charge of a warehouse section, have been considering making changes in the procedures to be followed in your section.   24._____
    While you are engaged in making this study, and in order to gain acceptance for any changes you might propose as a result of this study, it is generally MOST advisable for you to get comments and recommendations from

A. professional staff of the organization and planning unit of your department
B. storekeepers in charge of other sections of the warehouse who have made changes in their own sections
C. your subordinates who might be affected by any changes
D. your superior

25. Of the following positions, the one for which you may expect normally to have the greatest amount of difficulty in determining meaningful numerical work standards is a(n)

A. forklift operator
B. inventory clerk
C. order picker
D. watchman

KEY (CORRECT ANSWERS)

1. D
2. C
3. B
4. D
5. B

6. C
7. B
8. D
9. A
10. C

11. C
12. B
13. C
14. D
15. C

16. B
17. D
18. B
19. C
20. B

21. D
22. B
23. C
24. C
25. D

TEST 2

DIRECTIONS: Each question or incomplete statement is followed by several suggested answers or completions. Select the one that BEST answers the question or completes the statement. *PRINT THE LETTER OF THE CORRECT ANSWER IN THE SPACE AT THE RIGHT.*

1. In teaching new employees how to use forklift equipment, the BEST procedure to follow is:

    A. Give class lecture instructions and then let the employees use the equipment
    B. Let the employees try it themselves and then show them what they are doing wrong
    C. Show the employees how you use the equipment and then answer any questions they may have
    D. Tell the employees how to do it, give a demonstration, have the employees do it, and correct their mistakes

    1.____

2. Assume that you have assigned one of your assistant stockmen to perform a task involving several steps that he has never done before.
   In this situation, of the following, it is generally MOST important for you to

    A. check closely each step in the task as it is being performed or immediately after its completion
    B. make sure that the assistant stockman fully understands the last step before he starts the task
    C. make available to the assistant stockman any tools and equipment that he may request
    D. stress the importance of the task to the assistant stockman

    2.____

3. On the first morning that you report to work at a new job location as a newly-promoted supervisor of a small unit, your superior asks you what you would like to do FIRST.
   Of the following, the LEAST appropriate response for you to make is to say, *I'd like to*

    A. meet the employees who work in my unit
    B. recommend some changes in the procedures used in my unit
    C. obtain a manual of procedure, if one is available.
    D. see the physical area in which my unit works

    3.____

4. Assume that a storekeeper has assigned a laborer to assist a stockman in doing a certain task. The stockman reports to the storekeeper that the laborer has not been doing the work which he, the stockman, has been assigning him.
   The MOST appropriate action for the storekeeper to take FIRST in this situation is to

    A. direct the laborer to obey the instructions of the stockman
    B. have a conference with both the stockman and the laborer present
    C. reassign the laborer to another task
    D. speak to the laborer to get his side of the story

    4.____

5. Assume that you have received a delivery of sand, which took up the entire area of a trailer with interior dimensions of 40 feet by 7 feet, and the sand was loaded to an average depth of 4 feet.
The amount of storage space, in cubic yards, required for this shipment of sand is MOST NEARLY _____ cubic yards.

   A. 42   B. 125   C. 374   D. 1,120

6. Assume that lubricating oil is delivered to your warehouse in 20 gallon drums. Requisitions for amounts less than 20 gallons are filled by drawing off the required amount of lubricating oil from one of the 20 gallon drums. After filling several requisitions for various amounts of lubricating oil, you find that you have on hand 18 full drums, 6 drums that are three-quarters full, 4 drums that are one-half full, and 8 drums that are one-quarter full.
The total amount of lubricating oil that you have on hand is _____ gallons.

   A. 360   B. 530   C. 540   D. 600

7. Assume that your warehouse issues paint in gallon cans and in quart cans. At the beginning of a certain week, you have 150 gallon cans and 100 quart cans of paint on hand. On Monday, you issue 10 gallon cans and 9 quart cans; on Tuesday, 9 gallon cans and 4 quart cans; on Wednesday, 4 gallon cans and 7 quart cans; on Thursday, 7 gallon cans and 11 quart cans; and on Friday, you issue 5 gallon cans and 5 quart cans.
The total number of cans of paint on hand at the end of this week, assuming you have received no shipments of paint, is _____ gallon cans and _____ quart cans.

   A. 35; 36   B. 65; 64   C. 65; 86   D. 115; 64

8. A storage carton with dimensions of 1 foot 6 inches by 2 feet 4 inches by 4 feet has MOST NEARLY a volume of _____ cubic feet.

   A. 9.33   B. 10   C. 14   D. 15.36

9. Assume that you can purchase a gallon of turpentine for $1.70. A discount of 10% is given for purchases of 80 gallons or more.
If you purchase 100 gallons of turpentine, the unit cost of one QUART is MOST NEARLY _____ cents.

   A. 38   B. 43   C. 77   D. 85

10. Assume that you have dispatched a truck at 9 A.M. to make a single delivery at a location which is 20 miles from your warehouse.
Assuming that the truck travels at an average speed of 15 miles per hour and that one-half hour is required to make the delivery, you should expect the truck to return to the warehouse at approximately

    A. 10:50 A.M.   B. 11:40 A.M.
    C. 12:10 P.M.   D. 12:40 P.M.

11. Assume that you are informed that on the next day at 9 A.M. you will receive six truckloads of goods. Two man-hours are required to unload each truckload of goods, and 6 man-hours are required to place each truckload of goods in storage.
If you plan to complete this task by 1 P.M., the MINIMUM number of men that you should assign to this task is

    A. 4   B. 8   C. 12   D. 16

12. Assume that you have in stock 15 one-gallon cans of rubber cement thinner. After filling an order for 50 bottles each containing 16 fluid ounces of rubber cement thinner, the amount of rubber cement thinner remaining in stock is

   A. none; you do not have enough stock to fill this order
   B. 1 gallon 1 quart
   C. 4 gallons 1 1/2 quarts
   D. 8 gallons 3 quarts

13. Assume that you have been instructed to order mineral spirits as soon as the supply on hand falls to the level required for sixty days of issue.
    If the total amount of mineral spirits on hand is 960 gallons and you issue an average of 8 gallons of mineral spirits per day, and your warehouse works a five-day week, you will be required to order mineral spirits in _____ working days.

   A. 50   B. 60   C. 70   D. 80

Questions 14-17.

DIRECTIONS: Questions 14 through 17 are to be answered SOLELY or the basis of the information given below.

NUMBER OF SPECIAL ORDERS PICKED AND PACKED EACH DAY DURING. WEEK

Stockman A - Monday 20; Tuesday 20; Wednesday 25;
   Thursday 30; Friday 30

Stockman B - Monday 25; Tuesday 30; Wednesday 35;
   Thursday 20; Friday 35

Stockman C - Monday 15; Tuesday 20; Wednesday 25;
   Thursday 30; Friday 30

Stockman D - Monday 30; Tuesday 35; Wednesday 40;
   Thursday 35; Friday 40

14. Which stockman picked and packed a total of exactly 120 special orders during the week?
    Stockman

   A. A   B. B   C. C   D. D

15. The stockman who picked and packed the LEAST number of special orders on Thursday is Stockman

   A. A   B. B   C. C   D. D

16. The total number of special orders picked and packed during the week by all four stockmen is

   A. 125   B. 460   C. 560   D. 570

17. By what percentage did the number of orders picked and packed by Stockman C on Friday exceed the number of orders picked and packed by Stockman C on Monday?

   A. 15%   B. 30%   C. 100%   D. 200%

Questions 18-25.

DIRECTIONS: Questions 18 through 25 are to be answered SOLELY on the basis of the information given in the table below.

TABLE OF INFORMATION ABOUT GARDEN HOSE ON HAND

Commodity Index Number	Kind and Diameter of Hose (in inches)	Number of Feet Per Roll	Weight Per Roll lbs.	Weight Per Roll oz.	Cost Per Roll	Number of Rolls on Hand
SL 14171	Plastic, 3/4 in.	25	6	5	$5.90	20
SL 14172	Plastic, 3/4 in.	50	12	5	9.90	50
SL 14271	Plastic, 5/8 in.	25	4	7	4.40	40
SL 14272	Plastic, 5/8 in.	50	8	10	7.40	50
SL 14273	Plastic, 5/8 in.	75	13	0	10.40	50
SL 14274	Plastic, 5/8 in.	100	17	0	13.40	100
SL 24171	Rubber, Reinforced, 3/4"	25	9	3	8.90	20
SL 24172	Rubber, Reinforced 3/4"	50	18	0	14.90	10
SL 24271	Rubber, Reinforced, 5/8"	25	6	2	6.20	40
SL 24272	Rubber, Reinforced, 5/8"	50	12	2	10.90	40
SL 24273	Rubber, Reinforced, 5/8"	75	18	0	15.20	60
SL 24274	Rubber, Reinforced, 5/8"	100	24	0	19.90	100

18. The total weight of all of the 25 foot rolls of rubber, reinforced, 5/8 inch garden hose on hand is _____ lbs.

    A. 175   B. 240   C. 245   D. 485

19. Ah order for 10 rolls of SL 14271, 17 rolls of SL 14274, and 22 rolls of SL 24271 will MOST NEARLY weigh _____ lbs.

    A. 333   B. 423   C. 468   D. 472

20. The total cost of 12 rolls of 100 foot plastic, 5/8 inch garden hose is

    A. $124.80   B. $134.00   C. $160.80   D. $238.80

21. Assume that from the 40 rolls of SL 24272 and the 100 rolls of SL 24274, you ship one order of 10 rolls of SL 24272 and one order of 50 rolls of SL 24274.
    The total cost of all of the SL 24272 and the SL 24274 garden hose still on hand, after filling these orders, is

    A. $479   B. $1,104   C. $1,322   D. $1,451

22. Assume that 15% of all the 100 foot rolls of plastic garden hose and rubber reinforced garden hose are found defective.
    Then, the total cost of the defective hose is

    A. $199.00   B. $298.00   C. $333.00   D. $499.50

23. The stock on hand of which one of the following sizes and types of garden hose has the GREATEST total cost?
SL

    A. 14171   B. 14271   C. 24171   D. 24172

24. If 3/4 inch plastic garden hose is taken from the 50 foot rolls, then the cost of one foot of such hose is MOST NEARLY

    A. 20¢   B. 23¢   C. 26¢   D. 29¢

25. If it takes one worker one hour to inspect 20 rolls of garden hose for defects, the LEAST amount of time it will take two workers to inspect ALL the rolls of garden hose in stock is _____ hours _____ minutes.

    A. 14; 30   B. 15; 50   C. 24; 10   D. 29; 0

KEY (CORRECT ANSWERS)

1. D
2. A
3. B
4. D
5. A

6. B
7. D
8. C
9. A
10. C

11. C
12. D
13. B
14. C
15. B

16. D
17. C
18. C
19. C
20. C

21. C
22. D
23. C
24. A
25. A

EXAMINATION SECTION
TEST 1

DIRECTIONS: Each question or incomplete statement is followed by several suggested answers or completions. Select the one that BEST answers the question or completes the statement. *PRINT THE LETTER OF THE CORRECT ANSWER IN THE SPACE AT THE RIGHT.*

1. Assume that your warehouse received a shipment of 600 articles. A sample of 60 articles was inspected. Of this sample, one article was wholly defective, and four articles were partly defective. On the basis of this sampling, you would expect the total number of defective articles in this shipment to be

    A. 5   B. 10   C. 40   D. 50

    1.____

2. The stock inventory card for paint, white, flat, one gallon, has the following entries:

Date	Received	Shipped	Balance
April 12	-	25	75
April 13	50	75	
April 14	-	10	
April 15	25	-	
April 16	-	10	

    The balance on hand at the close of business on April 15 should be

    A. 40   B. 45   C. 55   D. 65

    2.____

Questions 3-8.

DIRECTIONS: For each Question 3 through 8, select the choice whose meaning is MOST NEARLY the same as that of the numbered item.

3. ADJACENT

    A. near   B. critical   C. sensitive   D. sharp

    3.____

4. CONSOLIDATE

    A. divide in half   B. direct
    C. agree   D. unite

    4.____

5. DETERIORATE

    A. decorate   B. prevent   C. regulate   D. worsen

    5.____

6. EXPEDITE

    A. label carefully   B. process promptly
    C. represent   D. terminate

    6.____

7. NEGLIGENT

    A. careless   B. painful   C. pleasant   D. positive

    7.____

8. VENDOR

    A. customer   B. inspector   C. manager   D. seller

    8.____

11

Questions 9-12.

DIRECTIONS: Questions 9 through 12 are to be answered SOLELY on the basis of the following passage.

Several special factors must be taken into account in selecting trucks to be used in a warehouse that stores food in freezer and cold storage rooms. Since gasoline fumes may contaminate the food, the trucks should be powered by electricity, not by gasoline. The trucks must be specially equipped to operate in the extreme cold of freezer rooms. The equipment must be dependable, for if a truck breaks down while transporting frozen food from a railroad car to the freezer of a warehouse, this expensive merchandise will quickly spoil. Finally, since cold storage and freezer rooms are expensive to operate, commodities must be stored close together, and the aisles between the rows of commodities must be as narrow as possible. Therefore, the trucks must be designed to work even in narrow aisles.

9. Of the following, the BEST title for the above passage is:

    A. Expenses Involved in Operating a Freezer or Cold Storage Room
    B. How to Prevent Food Spoilage in Freezer and Cold Storage Rooms
    C. Selecting the Best Trucks to Use in a Food Storage Warehouse
    D. The Problem of Contamination of Food by Gasoline Fumes

10. According to the above passage, electrically powered trucks should be used for moving food in freezer and cold storage rooms chiefly because they

    A. are cheaper to operate than gasoline powered trucks
    B. are dependable
    C. can operate in extremes of heat and cold
    D. do not produce fumes which may contaminate food

11. Trucks designed for use in narrow aisles should be used in freezer and cold storage rooms because

    A. commodities are placed close together in freezer rooms to save space
    B. commodities spoil quickly if the space between aisles in the freezer is too wide
    C. narrow aisle trucks are more dependable
    D. narrow aisle trucks are run by electricity

12. According to the above passage, all of the following factors should be taken into account in selecting a truck for use to transport frozen food into and within a cold storage room EXCEPT

    A. ability to operate in extreme cold
    B. dependability
    C. the weight of the truck
    D. whether or not the truck emits exhaust fumes

Questions 13-22.

DIRECTIONS: For Questions 13 through 22, choose from the given classifications the one under which the item is MOST likely to be found in general stock catalogs.

13. *Columnar pads* may BEST be classified under 13.____

    A. dry goods, textiles, and floor covering
    B. hospital and surgical supplies
    C. recreational supplies and equipment
    D. stationery and office supplies

14. *Trowels* may BEST be classified under 14.____

    A. dry goods and textiles
    B. hand tools and agricultural implements
    C. household supplies
    D. surgical supplies

15. *Collanders* may BEST be classified under 15.____

    A. building materials   B. kitchen utensils
    C. motor vehicle parts   D. plumbing supplies

16. *Litmus paper* may BEST be classified under 16.____

    A. laboratory supplies   B. sewing supplies
    C. stationery and supplies   D. textiles

17. *Pipettes* may BEST be classified under 17.____

    A. hardware
    B. hospital and laboratory supplies
    C. kitchen utensils and tableware
    D. plumbing fixtures and parts

18. *Carbon tetrachloride* may BEST be classified under 18.____

    A. brushes
    B. clothing and textiles
    C. drugs and chemicals
    D. toilet articles and accessories

19. *Curry powder* may BEST be classified under 19.____

    A. drugs and chemicals
    B. food and condiments
    C. paints and supplies
    D. surgical and dental supplies

20. *Wing nuts* may BEST be classified under 20.____

    A. food and condiments   B. hardware supplies
    C. household utensils   D. sewing supplies

21. *Shears* may BEST be classified under 21.____

    A. agricultural implements   B. clothing and textiles
    C. electrical parts   D. furniture

22. *Chambray* may BEST be classified under

    A. canned goods, food, and miscellaneous groceries
    B. brooms and brushes
    C. drugs and chemicals
    D. dry goods and textiles

23. Four city-owned trucks, all the same make, model, and capacity, were dispatched on round trips each with a 120 gallon tank full of gas. After Truck A had traveled 225 miles, his tank was 1/4 full. After Truck B had traveled 120 miles, his tank was 1/2 full. After Truck C had traveled 75 miles, his tank was 3/4 full. After Truck D had traveled 300 miles, his tank was empty. Which truck had the POOREST average mileage per gallon of gas?
    Truck

    A. A   B. B   C. C   D. D

24. Assume that you receive a shipment of 9 boxes of paper towels. Each box contains 6 dozen packages. Each package contains 200 paper towels. The total cost of the shipment of boxes is $64.80. The unit of issue for paper towels is the package.
    The unit cost of the paper towels is

    A. $0.10   B. $0.90   C. $1.20   D. $7.20

25. One shipment of 70 shovels costs $140. A second shipment of 130 shovels costs $208. The average cost per shovel for both shipments is MOST NEARLY

    A. $1.60   B. $1.75   C. $2.00   D. $2.50

KEY (CORRECT ANSWERS)

1. D
2. D
3. A
4. D
5. D

6. B
7. A
8. D
9. C
10. D

11. A
12. C
13. D
14. B
15. B

16. A
17. B
18. C
19. B
20. B

21. A
22. D
23. B
24. A
25. B

TEST 2

DIRECTIONS: Each question or incomplete statement is followed by several suggested answers or completions. Select the one that BEST answers the question or completes the statement. *PRINT THE LETTER OF THE CORRECT ANSWER IN THE SPACE AT THE RIGHT.*

Questions 1-5.

DIRECTIONS: Questions 1 through 5 show items that have been requisitioned by city agencies. In each group of four items, there is one item which has NOT been described in sufficient detail to enable the storekeeper or his subordinates to fill the order promptly from the variety of stock on hand. For each question, select the item that has pertinent, important information missing.

1. A. Fuses, auto, glass, 25 volts
   B. Ladders, extension, 2 sections, 30', metal
   C. Paint, interior, white, 1 gallon can, flat
   D. Stoppers, rubber, solid, white, nickel plated, brass ring, 1"

   1.____

2. A. Aspirin, U.S.P., 1 grain - 1,000 in bottle
   B. Blotters, desk, 120 lb. stock, 24" x 38", green
   C. Folders, file, manila, 1/3 cut
   D. Nutmeg, ground, 1 lb. container

   2.____

3. A. Safety pins, brass, nickel plated, size 2
   B. Sheets, bed, cotton, white
   C. Thermometer, oven, 100/600 degree F, enamel
   D. Toothbrush, adult size, nylon bristle

   3.____

4. A. Pencil, black lead, #2, general office use, with eraser
   B. Stencil, dry-process, blue, legal size #2960
   C. Tape, cellulose, 1/2 in. x 1296 in., core diameter 1 in.
   D. Typewriter ribbon, standard, black record

   4.____

5. A. Fruits, canned, peaches
   B. Milk, processed, dry powdered, whole, bulk
   C. Olives, stuffed, 16 oz. bottle, 12 bottles to case
   D. Sugar, granulated, 100 lb. bag

   5.____

6. The deterioration of some items is accelerated when temperature exceeds 70° F and humidity is greater than 40 percent.
   Of the following, the item that would be LEAST affected by increases of temperature and humidity above these amounts is

   A. bristle brushes   B. cellophane tape
   C. rice   D. typewriter ribbons

   6.____

7. The storage life of many items varies according to temperature and humidity.
   To gain maximum storage life, the one of the following items which should be stored in an area having a temperature of 55° F with 50 percent relative humidity is

   7.____

15

A. clothing B. steel parts
C. tires D. x-ray film

8. A shipment of 200 creosote logs 12" in diameter with lengths varying from 20' to 30' each will arrive on flatbed trucks and are to be stored. The mode of power to be employed to move the logs from the flatbeds to an outdoor storage area is a warehouse crane.
To avoid slippage, the pulley ropes or chains should be attached to the logs with a

   A. double basket sling
   B. double choker sling with hooks attached
   C. four leg bridle sling with spliced eyes
   D. hammock sling

Questions 9-12.

DIRECTIONS: Questions 9 through 12 represent items appearing on requisitions received in a storehouse. Assume that you have a wide variety of each item named. Some important information is missing from each description. Without this missing information (NOT code number or account number), it would be difficult to select the appropriate item from the variety in stock. From the choices given, select the one that represents the missing additional information that would be MOST important and helpful in filling each requisition.

9. PAPER, mimeograph, 100% sulphite sub 20, white

   A. bond or onionskin B. ruled or unruled
   C. size of paper D. two or three holes

10. NEEDLES, hand sewing, 20 to package

    A. cost B. metallic composition
    C. purpose D. size

11. SCREWS, wood, gross in box, brass, 1/2", No. 2

    A. round or flat head
    B. size of bolt
    C. type of lumber for which used
    D. type of metal of which made

12. THREAD, SPOOL COTTON, hand sewing, 6 cord, 500 yd., one dozen in box, #60

    A. color of thread
    B. size of needle's eye
    C. type of fabric to be sewn
    D. diameter of spool

13. Of the following, the LEAST appropriate preservative to apply to a wooden ladder is

    A. clear varnish B. lacquer
    C. linseed oil D. paint

14. Of the following, the type of lighting that is MOST efficient for maximum illumination in an equipment maintenance area is

    A. *incandescent* (direct)
    B. *incandescent* (general diffusing)
    C. *fluorescent* (direct)
    D. *fluorescent* (semi-direct)

15. Of the following chemicals, the one which is MOST hazardous and requires extra precautionary storage and handling methods is

    A. citric acid
    B. hydrogen peroxide
    C. nitric acid
    D. oxalic acid

16. You are informed that several cases of canned condensed milk have spoiled and you are assigned to seek the cause and find a remedy.
    In the absence of any specific information, which of the following is MOST likely to have been the cause of this spoilage?

    A. Improper rotation of stock
    B. Adequate ventilation
    C. Insect infestation
    D. Insufficient heat

17. Inventory records are essential to efficient warehouse operations.
    Of the following purposes served by inventory records, the one which is of LEAST importance to warehouse operating personnel is the

    A. establishment of quantity controls
    B. estimation of present values of items
    C. identification of stock items
    D. location of stock items

18. When in storage, the one of the following which it is MOST important to sprinkle periodically with naphthalene flakes is

    A. canvas cots
    B. cotton towels
    C. manila rope
    D. wool blankets

19. Generally, the time required to fill a requisition will be LEAST affected by the _____ of the item requisitioned.

    A. amount
    B. dimensions
    C. length of the description
    D. location

20. Of the following, the BEST procedure to follow in order to insure that a laborer has understood instructions that you have just given to him is to

    A. ask the laborer if he has any questions about the instructions
    B. have the laborer explain the instructions to you
    C. repeat the key points of the instructions to the laborer
    D. write out the instructions and give them to the laborer

21. You have been assigned several newly-appointed inexperienced stockmen and laborers whose performance in inadequate.
Of the following, the BEST course of action is to

    A. commence a training program for all employees under your supervision
    B. provide special guidance to those employees whose performance is inadequate
    C. do a work simplification study
    D. take steps to improve morale through incentive awards

22. Assume that one of your subordinates knows more about a certain aspect of the work than you do. You notice that many of the workers go to him rather than to you for advice on this aspect of the work.
You should

    A. delegate your authority and responsibility in this aspect of the work to this subordinate
    B. direct the workers to bring all questions about the work to you
    C. permit this to continue as long as it does not interfere with the work of this subordinate
    D. tell this subordinate that he is to refer any requests for information to you

23. Assume that about 11 A.M. one of your stockmen reports to you that one of the assistant stockmen appears to be drunk and is creating a disturbance in the warehouse. The MOST appropriate action for you to take FIRST in this situation is to

    A. ask the stockman to bring the assistant stockman who appears to be drunk to your office
    B. call the police department for assistance
    C. go with the stockman to investigate the matter
    D. report the matter to your supervisor

24. Assume that you have received an anonymous letter alleging that the crew of one of your delivery trucks has been observed parked at a certain location for periods of one hour or more on several occasions. This location is not in the vicinity of any agency where your crew would be required to make deliveries.
In this situation, the MOST appropriate action for you to take is to

    A. break up the crew by reassigning each member to other duties
    B. follow the crew for several days as they are making deliveries
    C. ignore the letter since it is anonymous
    D. interview each member of the crew privately to find out what he has to say about the allegation

25. Assume that one of your subordinates has gotten into the habit of regularly and routinely referring every small problem which arises in his work to you.
In order to help him overcome this habit, it is generally MOST advisable for you to

   A. advise him that you do not have time to discuss each problem with him and that he should do whatever he wants
   B. ask your subordinate for his solution and approve any satisfactory approach that he suggests
   C. refuse to discuss such routine problems with him
   D. tell him that he should consider looking for another position if he does not feel competent to solve such routine problems

---

KEY (CORRECT ANSWERS)

1.	A	11.	A
2.	C	12.	A
3.	B	13.	D
4.	D	14.	C
5.	A	15.	C
6.	A	16.	A
7.	D	17.	B
8.	B	18.	D
9.	C	19.	C
10.	D	20.	B

21. B
22. C
23. C
24. D
25. B

EXAMINATION SECTION
TEST 1

DIRECTIONS: Each question or incomplete statement is followed by several suggested answers or completions. Select the one that BEST answers the question or completes the statement. *PRINT THE LETTER OF THE CORRECT ANSWER IN THE SPACE AT THE RIGHT.*

Questions 1-10.

DIRECTIONS: Questions 1 through 10 are to be answered on the basis of Tables I and II below.

TABLE I
Building 5 Storeroom
Report of Dollar Cost of Stores Issued To
All Divisions in the Month of December

Divisions	11 Dept. Reports & Bulletins	12 Food Supplies	13 Motor Vehicle Supplies	14 Office Supplies	15 Printed Stationery & Forms	16 Printing & Reproducing Supplies	17 Small Tools & Implements
A	40		125	85	13	55	45
B	21		231	35	46	32	61
C	68	422		75	37	81	
D	81			83	98	77	91
E	32	168		69	51	43	

TABLE II
Building 5 Storeroom

Summary of Dollar Cost of Stores Issued
and Received and Balances, December

1 Supply Code	2 Balance Beginning of Month	3 Receipts From Vendors	4 Receipts From Storehouse A	5 Receipts From Storehouse B	6 Total Receipts	7 Total Issued	8 Balance
11	200	112	83	21	216	242	174
12	472	225	200	46	471	590	119
13	365	400			765	356	409
14	257	75	245	27	347	357	
15	245	89	152	36	277	255	277
16	281	104	190		294	288	287
17	197	32	110	40	182	197	182

2 (#1)

1. The average value of small tools and implements received by Division C and E during the month of December

   A. is zero
   B. is approximately 78
   C. is 197
   D. cannot be determined from the information given

2. The division which received the GREATEST dollar value of stores in the month of December was

   A. A   B. B   C. C   D. D

3. The division which received the GREATEST number of items in all supply categories in December

   A. is A
   B. is B
   C. is D
   D. cannot be determined from the information given

4. In the column *Total Issued*, the entry which is INCORRECT is for

   A. Food Supplies
   B. Motor Vehicle Supplies
   C. Office Supplies
   D. Printed Stationery & Forms

5. In the column *Total Receipts*, the entry which is INCORRECT is for

   A. Department Reports & Bulletins
   B. Motor Vehicle Supplies
   C. Office Supplies
   D. Small Tools & Equipment

6. The Balance for Supply Code 14 has been omitted. This figure should be

   A. 10   B. 247   C. 367   D. 594

7. The Balance has been INCORRECTLY entered for

   A. Department Reports and Bulletins
   B. Food Supplies
   C. Printing and Reproducing Supplies
   D. Small Tools and Equipment

8. The dollar value of department reports and bulletins received from vendors in December exceeds that received from the storehouses by

   A. 8   B. 12
   C. 29   D. an indeterminate amount

9. For the classes of items received from Storehouse B during the month of December, the average dollar cost of these classes was MOST NEARLY

   A. 24   B. 34   C. 65   D. 170

10. One space is left blank in Column 4 of Table II. Judging only from the above tables, the MOST probable reason for this is that   10.____
    A. motor vehicle supplies were obtained from vendors only
    B. number 365 was inadvertently omitted from Column 4
    C. the figures for Columns 4 and 5 were included in Column 3
    D. the motor vehicle supply stock of Storehouse A is below the minimum stock level

11. If a physical inventory reveals a much smaller number of a particular item than is shown by the perpetual inventory record, it PROBABLY indicates   11.____
    A. a discontinuation of the stocking of the item
    B. a failure to record a withdrawal on the inventory record
    C. an unusual consumption of that particular item
    D. the non-delivery of an order for that item

12. The number of cartons measuring 3' x 3' x 2' which will be needed to pack 1,728 boxed items each measuring   12.____
    3" x 9" x 6" is
    A. 9   B. 18   C. 108   D. 192

13. Assume that a storehouse floor is 300 feet long, 200 feet wide, and 10 feet high. The total weight that the floor can hold is 3,000 tons.   13.____
    The safe floor load is _____ pounds per square foot.
    A. 100   B. 200   C. 300   D. 600

14. Seventy cartons, each 2 feet wide, 3 feet long, and 4 feet high, will require storage space measuring APPROXIMATELY _____ cubic yards.   14.____
    A. 24   B. 56   C. 63   D. 187

15. A certain item is stored in a crate measuring 3 feet in length, 4 feet in width, and 6 inches in height. It weighs 60 pounds.   15.____
    If the usable height of the storage area is twelve feet and if the safe floor load is 140 pounds per square foot, the number of crates which may be stacked right side up in a single column is
    A. 2   B. 5   C. 11   D. 24

16. You have to load 5,000 items on trucks each having a maximum load capacity of 2 1/2 tons. Each item weighs 20 pounds and takes up 2 cubic feet of storage space. Assume that the storage space in each truck has an area of 68 square feet and is 6 feet high. Without exceeding space or weight limitations, the SMALLEST number of trucks that could be used is   16.____
    A. 20   B. 25   C. 50   D. 63

17. Twenty pallet loads of a certain commodity have to be unloaded from a truck and moved to a certain location in the storehouse. It takes a forklift truck five minutes to unload two pallet loads at one time and place them on a trailer which can hold four pallet loads. It takes one tractor ten minutes to move five loaded trailers to the proper location in the storehouse.
    Using one forklift truck, one tractor, and five trailers, and assuming no other time lost, the pallet loads can be unloaded and moved to the place where they will be stacked in

    A. 50 minutes
    B. 60 minutes
    C. 90 minutes
    D. 2 hours

18. A storeroom is 100 feet long and 26 feet wide. One aisle 8 feet wide runs the length of the storeroom. One aisle 4 feet wide runs the width of the storeroom.
    If there were no other aisles, the number of square feet of usable storage space would be

    A. 1,696 B. 1,728 C. 2,280 D. 2,568

19. A discount of 1% is given on all purchases of a certain item in quantities of 100 units or more. An additional discount of 1% is given on that portion of the purchase which exceeds 300.
    If 450 units are purchased at a list price of $6.00, the total cost is

    A. $2,619 B. $2,664 C. $2,670 D. $2,682

20. The amount of turpentine on hand is 27 1/2 gallons. One requisition is filled for 3 1/4 gallons, two additional requisitions are filled for 1 quart 8 ounces each, and five requisitions are filled for 2 pints 2 ounces each. The quantity of turpentine remaining after all these requisitions have been filled is

    A. 20 gal. 3 qts. 1 pt.
    B. 21 gal. 3 qts. 1 pt.
    C. 22 gal. 1 qt. 6 oz.
    D. 22 gal. 1 1/2 qts. 10 oz.

21. If the average height of the stacks in your section of the storehouse is 9 1/2 feet, the area which will be occupied by 11,400 cubic feet of supplies is APPROXIMATELY _____ square feet.

    A. 100 B. 120 C. 1,000 D. 1,200

22. Letting oily rags or dust cloths accumulate in a closet is a fire hazard PRINCIPALLY because of the possibility of

    A. a match or cigarette being dropped
    B. fire spreading from other areas
    C. spontaneous combustion
    D. their use in inflammable areas

23. Assume that you have depleted your entire stock of 1,692 units of a certain item by sending 524 units to one location and dividing the remainder of the stock equally among 16 other locations.
    The number of units that was sent to each of these 16 locations was

    A. 48 B. 73 C. 116 D. 168

24. Of the following, the MOST advisable way to increase storage space is to

    A. decrease stock supplies below minimum
    B. eliminate items that are infrequently used
    C. stack to maximum height
    D. utilize aisle space

25. In a large storehouse, an area with a high ceiling is ordinarily BEST for storing items which are

    A. irregular in shape, heavy, and on skids
    B. irregular in shape, light, and on pallets
    C. rectangular in shape and on pallets
    D. rectangular in shape and on skids

26. The term *legal-size* refers to paper which is generally _____ than letter-size paper.

    A. longer   B. longer and narrower
    C. longer and wider   D. wider

27. A *trier* is a device used for

    A. sampling   B. sealing   C. stamping   D. weighing

28. Of the following items, the one for which the MOST care should be taken to prevent moth damage is

    A. nylon brushes   B. orlon fabrics
    C. pianos   D. shoes

29. Circulation of air is LEAST desirable for

    A. batteries   B. cement   C. linoleum   D. paint

30. There are five units of a circular piece of equipment which weighs 9,000 pounds and has a solid circular base and a solid circular top each 4 feet in diameter.
    In MOST cases, the BEST way to store these five units would be to

    A. crate them and place one next to the other
    B. crate them and stack them two high
    C. place one next to the other without crating
    D. stack them two high without crating

31. You have just received a shipment of 500 packages, each 2" long, 1' wide, and 1/2' high, and each weighing 25 pounds. You are going to store them in an area 10' by 10' by 10' where the safe floor load is 100 pounds per square foot. The number of these packages which may be safely stored right side up is

    A. 100   B. 200   C. 400   D. 500

32. Assume that you have several men and the following equipment available: two forklift trucks, one tractor, five trailers, and two handtrucks.
    In order to move twenty pallet loads 200 yards in a storehouse, it would be MOST advisable for you to use the

A. forklift trucks
B. tractor and the trailers
C. tractor, the trailers, and the forklift trucks
D. tractor, the trailers, the handtrucks, and one fork-lift truck

33. Of the following, the MOST suitable temperature for the storage of fresh milk is   33._____

   A. 0° F   B. 16° F   C. 32° F   D. 48° F

34. Of the following, the MOST suitable temperature for the storage of frozen meats is   34._____

   A. 0° F   B. 16° F   C. 32° F   D. 48° F

35. An isolated section of the storehouse has just been made available for your use. It has all the facilities available in other sections of the storehouse, except that it is distant from shipping and receiving areas and all centers of activity.
Of the following items in the storehouse, the one which should ordinarily receive priority consideration for storage in such a section is   35._____

   A. codeine   B. flour   C. gasoline   D. machinery

36. Assume that you have to move 100 pallets from one location in the warehouse to another about 20 feet away. Which of the following would you need to do the job MOST efficiently?   36._____

   A. Conveyor
   B. Forklift truck
   C. Forklift truck, tractor, trailers
   D. Four-wheel handtruck, portable elevator

37. Of the following, the QUICKEST and EASIEST way to move thirty pallet loads of material 800 feet and then stack then is to use a   37._____

   A. forklift truck and a tractor-trailer train
   B. forklift truck and a crane
   C. portable elevator
   D. portable elevator and 6 handtrucks

38. The BEST measure of the effectiveness of a tractor-trailer combination is the   38._____

   A. amount of power used per day
   B. amount of stock that can be moved in a day
   C. amount of stock that can be moved in each trip
   D. number of miles which can be covered in a day

39. As compared to a conventional counterbalance design fork-lift truck, a straddle arm fork-lift truck with the same lifting capacity will USUALLY weigh   39._____

   A. approximately the same   B. less
   C. much more   D. slightly more

40. The one of the following which is NOT of major importance in determining the location of an item in a storehouse is   40._____

   A. difficulty of handling   B. fire hazard
   C. floor strength   D. purpose for which used

41. A usually competent stockman under your supervision has complained to you that a newly employed assistant stockman knows nothing about handling or storing stock.
    Of the following, the MOST advisable course of action for you to take is to

    A. advise the stockman not to interfere
    B. arrange for a transfer of the new worker
    C. ask the stockman whether he is willing to assist in on-the-job training
    D. tell the new worker that he will have to do better

42. Assume that an employee tells you that you have made an error in issuing certain instructions. You do not believe this to be true.
    The MOST appropriate action for you to take in MOST cases is to

    A. ask him to follow the instructions as they were given
    B. get some of the other employees together to discuss the matter
    C. have him explain why he believes it to be an error
    D. tell him to do it any way he wants to, as long as the job gets done

43. In planning a large operation involving the movement and handling of stock, it would be MOST desirable for a storekeeper to

    A. confer only with his supervisor and other storekeepers
    B. discuss the matter only with his more capable subordinates
    C. have his subordinates participate in the planning
    D. rely solely upon his own judgment and knowledge

44. As a storekeeper, you find that routine and clerical duties greatly decrease the time you can spend in supervising your subordinates.
    Of the following, you should FIRST attempt to

    A. delegate some of your supervisory duties to the most qualified subordinates
    B. have an assistant assigned to take over some of your duties
    C. reduce the number of persons under your supervision
    D. turn over some of the routine and clerical work to your subordinates

45. As a storekeeper in charge of a storehouse, you find that there is a considerable backlog in the filling of requisitions, and you have received complaints from using agencies Of the following, the MOST advisable course of action for you to take FIRST is to

    A. advise the using agencies that they must wait their turn
    B. determine the factors causing the backlog
    C. take appropriate disciplinary action where indicated
    D. work out plans for removing the backlog

46. It is necessary for you to assign one of the men in the storehouse to the main office for two weeks to work on records.
    Which of the following men should be chosen?

    A. Al is the best at records work, but he is very reluctant to go.
    B. Ben is next to Al in ability of records work and is interested in going, but he is so likeable that you are afraid the main office will want to keep him permanently.

C. Carl is next to Ben in ability at records work, but it would be a great hardship for him to go because of his time schedule and the traveling.
D. Dan has little ability at records work, but he has not done well in your division and he is anxious to try working in the main office.

47. An employee under your supervision comes to you to complain about an assignment you have made. You consider the matter to be unimportant, but it seems to be very important to him. He is excited and very angry.
Of the following, the MOST advisable action to take FIRST is to

   A. let him talk until he *gets it off his chest*
   B. refuse to talk to him until he has *cooled down*
   C. show him at once how unimportant the matter is
   D. tell him to talk it over with the other employees

48. Of the following, the BEST reason why accuracy in keeping records should be considered more important than speed is that

   A. most employees cannot work rapidly and also be accurate
   B. most supervisors insist upon accurate work, while very few pay attention to speed
   C. much time may be lost correcting or redoing work that is done too hastily
   D. speedy workers are usually inaccurate

49. A fistfight develops between two stockmen under your supervision.
The MOST advisable course of action for you to take FIRST is to

   A. call the police
   B. have the other workers pull them apart
   C. order them to stop
   D. step between the two men

50. You have assigned some difficult and unusual work to one of your most experienced and competent subordinates.
If you notice that he is doing the work incorrectly, you should

   A. assign the work to another employee
   B. reprimand him in private
   C. show him immediately how the work should be done
   D. wait until the job is completed and then correct his errors

KEY (CORRECT ANSWERS)

1. A	11. B	21. D	31. D	41. C
2. C	12. A	22. C	32. A	42. C
3. D	13. A	23. B	33. C	43. C
4. D	14. C	24. C	34. A	44. D
5. B	15. D	25. C	35. C	45. B
6. B	16. B	26. A	36. B	46. B
7. B	17. B	27. A	37. A	47. A
8. A	18. B	28. C	38. B	48. C
9. B	19. B	29. B	39. B	49. C
10. A	20. C	30. C	40. D	50. C

EXAMINATION SECTION
TEST 1

DIRECTIONS: Each question or incomplete statement is followed by several suggested answers or completions. Select the one that BEST answers the question or completes the statement. *PRINT THE LETTER OF THE CORRECT ANSWER IN THE SPACE AT THE RIGHT.*

1. The stock items on the purchase order should be the same as those on the shipment receipt at time of delivery. In general, it is BEST to check this at the time that the stock items are

    A. received in the storehouse
    B. ordered by the agency using the material
    C. issued by the storehouse personnel
    D. certified for payment

    1.____

2. Sawdust and shredded paper are materials that are generally used in *which one* of the following operations?

    A. Packing   B. Inventory   C. Spraying   D. Transporting

    2.____

3. Storage areas with good air circulation and ventilation are generally considered

    A. *good;* only in hot and humid weather
    B. *good;* to retard mold growth
    C. *poor;* due to danger of fire
    D. *poor;* because of cleaning costs

    3.____

4. To get the best use from storage areas, it is usually *desirable* to use high ceilinged areas for storing

    A. heavy bulky stock items
    B. light-weight stock items
    C. loose stock items in small bins
    D. extremely large sized stock items

    4.____

5. The section of the storeroom that can carry the least weight should generally NOT be used for storing stock items that

    A. have a large size
    B. have a small size
    C. are very heavy
    D. are very light

    5.____

6. Where should you store unusually large and heavy stock items, that are used very often?

    A. As close to the shipping and receiving areas as possible
    B. Away from work areas such as shipping and receiving
    C. On hand trucks until the using agency asks for the item
    D. Only in storage areas which are outside the storehouse

    6.____

7. Which of the following would be MOST important in deciding how wide the space should be between cartons stacked in a storage area?

    A. Type of equipment that will be used to handle the stock
    B. Size of the storage area
    C. Number of employees in the storage area
    D. How far the storage area is away from the receiving area

    7.____

31

8. Stock items that might break, chip, or be crushed should be packed

   A. *tightly* with items touching each other
   B. *loosely* in a heavy wood container
   C. *tightly* with little movement allowed between items
   D. *tightly* with cushioning material between items

9. Suppose that some stock items delivered by truck are found to tie damaged before they are unloaded. Which of the following actions would be BEST to take?

   A. Take the damaged stock and then give it out first to prevent further damage
   B. Refuse to take any damaged items
   C. Tell the driver of the truck to return the entire shipment
   D. Tell your supervisor about the damage so that he can take the necessary steps

10. It is dangerous to store gasoline because

    A. it can only be stored in specially constructed rooms in a storehouse
    B. it gives off vapors that can easily burn
    C. it can explode when moved around
    D. no one has found a safe way of storing gasoline

11. Gases are usually stored under pressure in steel cans. Which of the following is the LEAST dangerous practice?

    A. Allowing the cans to come in contact with electrical circuits
    B. Lifting the cans by their valves
    C. Allowing the cans to touch each other
    D. Keeping the valves on the cans open after the gas has been used up

12. Acids are a danger in storage because leakage may result in a sudden fire if contact is made with other chemicals.
    When storing acids, the *one* of the following practices which is INCORRECT is to

    A. keep them in heavy duty metal cans
    B. store them in isolated areas
    C. protect the containers against breakage
    D. keep flames or lit matches out of areas where acids are stored

13. Tape with a cellophane backing will become wrinkled and lumpy if stored in an area that is

    A. warm   B. cool   C. damp   D. very dry

14. To keep wooden furniture from warping and twisting, it should be stored in an area that is

    A. warm and dry   B. warm and damp
    C. cool and dry   D. cool and damp

15. Which one of the following items should NOT be stored in a very dry storage area?

    A. Soup cubes   B. Baking soda
    C. Tea leaves   D. Lettuce

16. Suppose that a stockroom started the week with an initial supply of 3 gross of pencils and that one gross equals 144 pencils. After orders were filled, the stockroom had an inventory at the end of the week as follows: 2 gross of 4H pencils; 3 dozen 2B pencils, 1 1/2 dozen HB pencils, and 15 H pencils.
   How many pencils were ordered?

   A. 22 pencils   B. 45 pencils   C. 75 pencils   D. 97 pencils

17. How many 18-inch pieces can be cut from 10 lengths of 8-foot glass tubing?

   A. 47 pieces   B. 50 pieces   C. 53 pieces   D. 56 pieces

18. Suppose a roll of wire is 27 feet 3 inches long. A piece of wire measuring 18 feet 9 inches in length is cut from the roll.
    What is the length of wire left on the roll?

    A. 7 feet 3 inches   B. 7 feet 6 inches
    C. 8 feet 3 inches   D. 8 feet 6 inches

19. Suppose that 25% of a delivery of canned peaches was spoiled. If 36 cans were spoiled, then the delivery had a total of

    A. 9 cans   B. 25 cans   C. 144 cans   D. 180 cans

20. Suppose that a one-quart can of white flat ceiling paint weighs 5 pounds. What is the GREATEST number of quart cans that can be stored on a shelf that supports 167 pounds?

    A. 5 quart cans   B. 33 quart cans
    C. 41 quart cans   D. 67 quart cans

Questions 21-25.

DIRECTIONS: Answer Questions 21 through 25 on the basis of the formation given below.

LISTING OF PAPER				
Description	Quantity Ordered by Stockroom A (In dozen reams)	Quantity in Stock Before Delivery (In dozen reams)	Cost Per Ream	Location of Stock in Stockroom
8 1/2"x11" Blue	17	5	$ .94	Bin A7
8 1/2"x11" Buff	8	3	$ .93	Bin A7
8 1/2"x11" Green	11	4	$ .95	Bin B4
8 1/2"x11" Pink	10	4	$ .93	Bin B4
8 1/2"x11" White	80	15	$ .86	Bin A8
8 1/2"x13" White	76	12	$1.02	Bin A8
8 1/2"x14" Blue	7	2	$1.19	Bin A7
8 1/2"x14" Buff	7	3	$1.18	Bin A7
8 1/2"x14" Green	5	2	$1.20	Bin B4
8 1/2"x14" Pink	8	4	$1.18	Bin B4
8 1/2"x14" White	110	28	$1.15	Bin A8
8 1/2"x14" Yellow	2	1	$1.23	Bin C6

21. How many reams of 8 1/2"x13" paper will there be in stock if only one-half of the amount ordered is delivered?　　　21.____

    A. 456 reams　　B. 600 reams　　C. 912 reams　　D. 1056 reams

22. Suppose all ordered material is delivered. The bin that will have the MOST reams of paper is　　　22.____

    A. A7　　B. A8　　C. B4　　D. C6

23. Suppose all ordered material has been delivered. What is the approximate value of all 8 1/2"x11" paper which is in Bin B4?　　　23.____

    A. $27　　B. $171　　C. $198　　D. $327

24. How many reams of white paper of all sizes were ordered?　　　24.____

    A. 55 reams　　B. 266 reams　　C. 660 reams　　D. 3192 reams

25. Before any of the orders were delivered, the following requests were filled and removed from the stockroom:　　　25.____
    2 dozen reams 8 1/2" X 11" Blue; 2 dozen reams 8 1/2" X 11" Green;
    7 dozen reams 8 1/2" X 11" White; 5 dozen reams 8 1/2" x13" White;
    1 dozen reams 8 1/2" X 14" Green; 13 dozen reams 8 1/2" X14" Whit.
    How many reams of paper were left in the stockroom after the above requests were filled?

    A. 30　　B. 53　　C. 636　　D. 996

KEY (CORRECT ANSWERS)

1. A　　11. C
2. A　　12. A
3. B　　13. C
4. B　　14. C
5. C　　15. D

6. A　　16. C
7. A　　17. B
8. D　　18. D
9. D　　19. C
10. B　　20. B

21. B
22. B
23. D
24. D
25. C

TEST 2

DIRECTIONS: Each question or incomplete statement is followed by several suggested answers or completions. Select the one that *BEST* answers the question or completes the statement. *PRINT THE LETTER OF THE CORRECT ANSWER IN THE SPACE AT THE RIGHT.*

Questions 1-10.

DIRECTIONS: Each of Questions 1 through 10 presents a stock item followed by 4 classes of things. For each question choose the class of things in which the given item is *MOST* likely to be found.

1. *Pliers* may *BEST* be classified under 1.____

   A. food products
   B. tools
   C. office supplies
   D. machinery

2. *White Pine lumber* may *BEST* be classified under 2.____

   A. building materials
   B. laboratory materials
   C. safety materials
   D. seeds and plants

3. *Linseed oil* may *BEST* be classified under 3.____

   A. drugs and chemicals
   B. painters' supplies
   C. building materials
   D. fuel and fuel oils

4. *Ceiling tiles* may *BEST* be classified under 4.____

   A. office supplies
   B. hardware
   C. electrical supplies
   D. building materials

5. *Floor finish remover* may *BEST* be classified under 5.____

   A. insecticides
   B. drugs
   C. machinery
   D. cleaning supplies

6. *Arm slings* may *BEST* be classified under 6.____

   A. hospital supplies
   B. clothing
   C. school supplies
   D. office supplies

7. *Staplers* may *BEST* be classified under 7.____

   A. office supplies
   B. laboratory supplies
   C. machinery and metals
   D. engineering supplies

8. *Canvas stretcher* may *BEST* be classified under 8.____

   A. laboratory apparatus   B. hospital supplies   C. clothing

9. *Switches* may *BEST* be classified under 9.____

   A. camera supplies
   B. vehicles
   C. electrical supplies
   D. pipes and pipe fittings

35

10. *Bandages* may *BEST* be classified under

    A. laboratory equipment
    B. surgical instruments
    C. hospital supplies
    D. hose and belting

11. Employees who must lift and carry stock items should be careful to avoid injury. When an employee lifts or carries stock items, **which** of the following is the *LEAST* safe practice?

    A. Keep the legs straight and lift with the back muscles
    B. Keep the load as close to the body as possible
    C. Get a good grip on the object to be carried
    D. First determine if the item can be lifted and carried safely

12. For warning and protection, the color red is *usually* used for

    A. indicating high temperature stockroom areas
    B. floor markings
    C. location of first-aid supplies
    D. stop buttons, lights for barricades and other dangerous locations

13. Reporting rattles, squeaks, or other noises in equipment to your maintenance supervisor is

    A. *bad;* too much attention to squeaks like these keep important safety problems from being noticed
    B. *bad;* each person should oil and care for his own equipment
    C. *good;* these sounds may mean that the equipment should be fixed
    D. *good;* it shows the supervisor that you are a good worker

14. If you often get cuts on your hands from handling different kinds of cartons and boxes, the *BEST* thing for you to do is to

    A. keep from handling those kinds of cartons and boxes
    B. ask that better boxes and cartons be used
    C. toughen up your hands
    D. wear protective gloves

15. A low, movable platform used for stacking materials in a warehouse is called a "pallet". When lifting and moving "pallets" with a forklift, how should a stockman place the forks?

    A. As wide apart as possible
    B. As close together as possible
    C. Close together and tilted forward
    D. Wide apart and tilted forward

16. Suppose that 3-foot-high boxes are to be stacked in one pile on a 4-inch platform. In addition, 4-inch thick separators are placed between each layer of boxes. Suppose that the ceiling is 22 feet high and there must be at least 1 1/2 feet of space between the ceiling and the stacked boxes.
    What is the *GREATEST* number of boxes that can be stacked?

    A. 4   B. 5   C. 6   D. 7

17. A part of a storeroom measures 14 1/2 feet by 6 1/4 feet. The number of square feet in this part is

    A. 8 1/4 square feet   B. 20 3/4 square feet
    C. 90 5/8 square feet   D. 94 3/4 square feet

18. How many cubic feet of storage space would be taken up by 20 boxes, when each box measures 2 feet high, 2 feet wide, and 3 feet long?

    A. 12 cubic feet   B. 27 cubic feet
    C. 140 cubic feet   D. 240 cubic feet

19. Suppose that a truckload of canned items has been unloaded. There are six rows of boxes with seven boxes in each row. Each box has two dozen cans in it.
How many cans are there all together?

    A. 24   B. 144   C. 510   D. 1008

20. Suppose that the average weekly use of tissue amounts to 180 rolls.
At least how many boxes must be ordered for a 4-week period if there are 144 rolls in each box?

    A. 2   B. 3   C. 4   D. 5

Questions 21-25.

DIRECTIONS: Answer Questions 21 through 25 SOLELY on the basis of the information given in the table on the next page.

CONTROLLED DRUG A				
Time Period	Purchase Order Number and	Quantity Ordered	*Quantity Delivered by Vendor	Quantity Distributed during 2-Wk Period	Inventory Balance at end of 2-Wk period
April 23-May 6	110,327	105 ounces	135 ounces	27 ounces	108 ounces
May 7-May 20	111,437	42 ounces	40 ounces	39 ounces	109 ounces
May 21-June 3	112,347	37 ounces	27 ounces	32 ounces	104 ounces
June 4-June 17	112,473	35 ounces	35 ounces	45 ounces	94 ounces
June 18-July 1	114,029	40 ounces	40 ounces	37 ounces	97 ounces

*Delivery is made on first day of time period.

21. The difference between Quantity Ordered and Quantity Delivered was GREATEST on Purchase Order Number

    A. 110,327   B. 111,437   C. 112,347   D. 112,473

22. The difference between the total number of ounces ordered and the total number of ounces delivered on April 23 through June 18 is

    A. 17 ounces   B. 18 ounces   C. 19 ounces   D. 20 ounces

23. Suppose that average weekly usage was expected to be 26 ounces per week. Your supervisor has asked you to tell him whenever inventory balances get below a four-week level. Under these conditions, you should have told your supervisor during the two-week period beginning

    A. April 23, May 21, June 4, June 18
    B. May 21, June 4, June 18
    C. May 21, June 18
    D. June 4, June 18

23.___

24. The *GREATEST* decreases in inventory balances happened between the two-week periods beginning

    A. April 23 and May 7   B. May 7 and May 21
    C. May 21 and June 4   D. June 4 and June 18

24.___

25. Suppose a new program has been started at your hospital and the weekly usage of Drug A is expected to be 52 ounces per week. If your supervisor must keep on hand a four-week supply, then the amount that should be delivered for the two-week period beginning on July 2 is

    A. 52 ounces   B. 111 ounces   C. 208 ounces   D. 211 ounces

25.___

KEY (CORRECT ANSWERS)

1.	B	11.	B
2.	A	12.	D
3.	B	13.	C
4.	D	14.	D
5.	D	15.	A
6.	A	16.	C
7.	A	17.	C
8.	B	18.	D
9.	C	19.	D
10.	C	20.	D

21. A
22. C
23. D
24. C
25. B

EXAMINATION SECTION
TEST 1

DIRECTIONS: Each question or incomplete statement is followed by several suggested answers or completions. Select the one that BEST answers the question or completes the statement. *PRINT THE LETTER OF THE CORRECT ANSWER IN THE SPACE AT THE RIGHT.*

1. Of the following, the hazard MOST likely to damage rubber tubes in storage is

    A. breakage
    B. combustion
    C. corrosion
    D. deterioration

2. Of the following, the hazard MOST likely to damage vacuum tubes in storage is

    A. breakage
    B. corrosion
    C. deterioration
    D. evaporation

3. In checking large numbers of incoming supplies of a single item, the BEST practice to follow is to

    A. count the total number of containers received and only count the number of units in some of the containers
    B. count the total number of containers received only in those shipments where there is some doubt
    C. open all exterior containers received and count the number of containers inside when there are interior containers
    D. open all exterior and interior containers received and count the exact number of units

4. Some experts advise that barrels containing liquids should be turned occasionally. The BEST reason for this is to

    A. enable a check of the condition of the barrel
    B. enable a check of the condition of the contents
    C. keep the contents well mixed
    D. prevent the wood from drying out

5. For day-to-day protection when working in a room or enclosure containing combustible or explosive gases or gasolines, it would be MOST advisable to wear

    A. a general purpose gas mask
    B. a synthetic rubber suit
    C. non-sparking shoes
    D. rubber-framed goggles

6. The one of the following which is NOT recommended as a method of reducing the possibility of spontaneous combustion of burlap bags is to

    A. air them out before stacking
    B. dampen them slightly before stacking
    C. keep them off concrete floors
    D. keep them away from brick walls

39

7. When oxygen is leaking from a gas cylinder and the valve cannot close properly, the MOST advisable course of action to take while waiting for the valve to be repaired is to

    A. evacuate the building
    B. have it sent to a using agency before more oxygen is lost
    C. place the cylinder in the room with the poorest ventilation
    D. remove the cylinder from the building

7.____

8. Assume that you have to move four cartons to a location about 35 feet away. Each carton weighs 20 pounds and measures 2' x 8' x 4'.
   Of the following, the method of moving the cartons which would ordinarily be BEST is to

    A. have a team of two men make four trips
    B. have two teams of two men each carry two cartons
    C. make one trip using a four-wheel handtruck
    D. make one trip using a two-wheel handtruck

8.____

9. Assume that you have to move one carton to a location about 15 feet away. The carton weighs about 30 pounds and measures 8" x 18" x 24".
   Of the following, the method of moving the carton which would ordinarily be BEST is to

    A. have one man carry it
    B. have two men carry it
    C. put it on a two-wheel handtruck
    D. put it on a four-wheel handtruck

9.____

10. Assume that you have to move ten 45-pound cartons to a location about 75 feet away. Each carton measures 24" x 24" x 24".
    Of the following, the method of moving the cartons which would ordinarily be BEST is to

    A. load them on a pallet and use a forklift truck
    B. load them on a skid and push the skid
    C. load them on a trailer and pull it with a tractor
    D. use a portable conveyor

10.____

Questions 11-16.

DIRECTIONS: Questions 11 through 16 are to be answered SOLELY on the basis of the following table.

REPORT OF SEMI-ANNUAL INVENTORY

Article	Unit	Physical Inventory Qty.	Price	Amt.	Perpetual Inventory Qty.	Amt.	Adjustment Qty.	Amt.
Batteries, flashlight	ea.	63	.08	5.04	60	14.80	+3	+.24
Bolts, flat head with square nuts, 100 in box	box	23	1.47	33.80	25	36.75		
Fuse, 15 amp, 4 in box	box	80	.07	5.60	80	5.60		
Fuse, 20 amp, 4 in box	box	77	.07	5.39	80	5.60	3	.21
Tape, friction, 50 ft. to a roll	roll	45	.22	9.90	45	9.90		
Washers, 100 in can 1/8" beveled	can	35	.32	11.20	35	11.20		
3/8" beveled	can	41	.33	13.53	45	14.85	4	1.32
Totals				84.47		88.70		

11. In the above report, for which item is there an INCORRECT entry?   11._____

    A. 15 amp. fuses B. Friction tape
    C. Flashlight batteries D. 1/8" washers

12. In the above report, adjustments were omitted for _____ article(s).   12._____

    A. one B. two C. three D. four

13. After all appropriate entries have been made in the Adjustment column, the total which must be deducted from the book value of the inventory is   13._____

    A. $1.53 B. $1.77 C. $4.23 D. $4.71

14. The quantities shown in Perpetual Inventory exceed those shown in Physical Inventory by a total of   14._____

    A. 4 B. 6 C. 10 D. 12

15. The cost of ten washers, 1/8" beveled, is MOST NEARLY   15._____

    A. $.003 B. $.032 C. $.320 D. $3.20

16. The cost of 24 fuses is MOST NEARLY   16._____

    A. $.28 B. $.42 C. $.80 D. $1.68

17. Assume that you are in charge of a group of four men who are to carry an oak beam measuring 8" x 8" x 18' from one point to another.
    Of the following, the BEST method of carrying the beam is to have

    A. the men arrange themselves at equal distances along one side of the beam and carry the beam at their sides
    B. the men arrange themselves at equal distances on opposite sides of the beam and carry the beam at waist height
    C. the men arrange themselves in order of height along the beam so that the beam may be carried on the shoulders of all of the men
    D. two men stand at one end of the beam and two men at the other end in order to lift the beam on to the shoulders of the two strongest men

18. Although the old model of a certain item has been replaced by a new model which is interchangeable with the old model, most requisitions call specifically for the old model. Since your stock of the old model is almost depleted, it would be MOST advisable for you to

    A. establish a carefully regulated system of priorities based on need
    B. inform the source of your supply of the continued demand for the old model
    C. inform the using agencies or individuals of the feasibility of substituting the new model
    D. substitute the new model whenever the old model is called for

19. An assistant stockman is assigned by you to take physical inventory of a particular small part stored in several open boxes. This part is of uniform size and is packaged 100 to a box. He returns in an unusually short time with the count. His explanation for his speed is that he consolidated all the items as much as possible so that all except one box were full. He multiplied 100 by the number of boxes and added the number of additional parts left.
    Of the following, the MOST advisable course of action for you to take is to

    A. compliment him on his efficiency
    B. explain the proper way of taking inventory
    C. have him watch a more experienced worker take inventory
    D. suggest that he ask permission before changing procedure

20. In determining the number of months of supply to be ordered at one time, the LEAST important of the following factors is the

    A. average market price
    B. deterioration rate
    C. discount for quantity
    D. money available for purchasing

21. A check during physical inventory has revealed that many of the bottles of alcohol do not contain sixteen ounces as indicated on the labels.
    Of the following, the MOST advisable action to take FIRST is to

    A. check future shipments by the vendor immediately upon their arrival
    B. see if the bottles are tightly capped
    C. see if the cartons are wet
    D. question your subordinates about the situation

22. Of the following, the FIRST thing which should be done in order to determine the reason for a discrepancy between the perpetual inventory card and the bin card or other similar record is to

    A. check the original requisitions
    B. compare each transaction listed on both cards
    C. ascertain whether any stock has been transferred to another warehouse
    D. question all personnel involved

23. Items such as tools are sometimes issued on a temporary basis and are to be returned after use so that they may be issued again when needed. In such cases, a record of each withdrawal

    A. need not be kept
    B. should be made on an inventory card
    C. should be made on a locator card
    D. should be made on a separate register

24. Assume that you have 100 boxes of a particular item on hand. Since this is the minimum order point, you have already ordered 300 boxes, which is the usual 6 months' supply. This order has not yet been delivered, and you have just received a requisition for 1,000 boxes.
    Of the following, the MOST advisable action for you to take FIRST is to

    A. order an additional 1,000 boxes
    B. order an additional 1,300 boxes
    C. ascertain the reason for such a requisition
    D. inform the ordering agency that the requisition cannot be filled immediately

Questions 25-27.

   DIRECTIONS: Questions 25 through 27 are based on the following method of obtaining a reorder point: multiply the monthly rate of consumption by the lead time (in months) and add the minimum balance.

25. If the reorder point is 250 units, the lead time is 2 months, and the average monthly rate of consumption is 75 units, then the minimum balance is _____ units.

    A. 75　　　　B. 100　　　　C. 150　　　　D. 250

26. If the lead time is 30 days, the minimum balance is 200 units, and the average monthly rate of consumption is 100 units, then the reorder point is _____ units.

    A. 100　　　　B. 200　　　　C. 300　　　　D. 400

27. If the reorder point is 300 units, the lead time is 2 months, and the minimum balance is 100 units, then the average monthly rate of consumption is _____ units.

    A. 50　　　　B. 100　　　　C. 200　　　　D. 300

28. You are planning to submit an initial order for a new item. You estimate that you will issue 100 per month, and you want to have a two-month supply in reserve. You will reorder this item every six months. Your initial order should be for

    A. 200　　　　B. 600　　　　C. 700　　　　D. 800

29. For a particular item, the reorder point is established at 585. If the average rate of consumption is 130 and the lead time is 3 months, then the amount which should be on hand when the new delivery is received is

   A. 130   B. 195   C. 260   D. 325

30. You have room in the storehouse for 750 cartons of a certain item. Assume that you issue 125 cartons per month and keep a one-month supply in reserve. Delivery time is thirty days.
   Which of the following would it be MOST appropriate to order under these conditions?
   _____ every _____ months.

   A. 250; 3   B. 500; 3   C. 375; 4   D. 500; 4

31. Using maximum loads when transporting stock is

   A. *desirable* because it results in fewer trips
   B. *desirable* because it simplifies accounting and clerical work
   C. *undesirable* because it shortens the life of the equipment
   D. *undesirable* because it strains the capacity of the workers

32. Of the following, the BEST single basis for determining the desirability of purchasing new stock-handling equipment is the

   A. ability of the workers to handle the equipment
   B. condition of the present equipment
   C. estimated savings in costs
   D. size of the warehouse or stock facility

33. Frequent rest periods are MOST desirable when

   A. the men have been doing a good job
   B. the morale of the men is low
   C. there is a great deal of heavy work
   D. there is not too much work

34. In terms of plant economy, a storehouse is operating at GREATEST efficiency when it stores _____ stock that it is designed to hold.

   A. 10% less   B. 10% more
   C. 50% more   D. the exact amount of

35. Of the following, the one which a foreman or supervisor can MOST readily increase or improve is an employee's ability to

   A. get along with his fellow workers
   B. perform technical aspects of his job
   C. supervise others
   D. use good judgment in unusual situations

36. On one day, a certain piece of stock-handling equipment is not used at all. On the next day, several men are waiting to use it.
   This situation can BEST be corrected by

   A. having the men do the work manually
   B. keeping additional equipment available

C. posting a schedule for the use of the equipment
D. rearranging the work of the men

37. Despite all your efforts to streamline the work and make it more efficient, there still seems to be more work than you and your men can handle in a normal work week.
The MOST advisable course of action for you to take FIRST is to

   A. discuss the matter with your supervisor
   B. request more mechanical equipment
   C. request permission for overtime work
   D. tell your men that everyone will have to work a little harder

38. Assume that a subordinate tells you that he has made a mistake in filling out certain records.
The MOST advisable action for you to take FIRST is to

   A. explain how the job should have been done
   B. get another subordinate to do the job correctly
   C. tell him how to correct his mistake
   D. tell him to forget it but to do it correctly next time

39. Your supervisor gives you instructions which you feel are contrary to good storage procedure.
The MOST advisable action for you to take FIRST is to

   A. attempt to get additional support for your point of view
   B. follow his instructions without question
   C. suggest your method of doing the work
   D. say nothing but do the job the way you feel it should be done

40. You have reason to believe that one of your men is taking home merchandise from the storehouse. You question the man about this. He shows you that it was obsolete material of no value which was not salvageable and was about to be discarded.
Under these circumstances, the MOST appropriate action for you to take is to

   A. have him return the merchandise
   B. report the matter to your supervisor
   C. say nothing further
   D. tell the man that he should have asked your permission

41. Three new men have just been assigned to work under your supervision. Every time you give them an assignment, one of these men asks you several questions.
Of the following, the MOST advisable action for you to take is to

   A. assure him of your confidence in his ability to carry out the assignment correctly without asking so many questions
   B. have all three men listen to your answers to these questions
   C. point out that the other two men do the job without asking so many questions
   D. tell him to see if he can get the answers from other workers before coming to you

42. One of the men in your crew has continually been making derogatory statements about the personal life of one of the other men.
Of the following, it would probably be MOST advisable for you to

    A. attempt to obtain a transfer for the man who is the subject of the derogatory statements
    B. ignore the matter unless it has any effect on the work
    C. point out to your crew some of the weak spots in the character of the man who is making derogatory statements
    D. tell the man to stop making derogatory statements

43. Two of your subordinates suggest that you recommend a third man for an above-standard service rating because of his superior work.
You should

    A. ask the two subordinates whether the third man knows that they intended to discuss this matter with you
    B. explain to the two subordinates that an above-standard service rating for one man would have a detrimental effect on many of the other men
    C. recommend the man for an above-standard service rating if there is sufficient justification for it
    D. tell the two subordinates that the matter of service ratings is not their concern

44. At a meeting with your subordinates, which you have called in order to determine the best ways of dealing with some departmental policies, some of the men interrupt with comments and suggestions.
Of the following, the MOST advisable course of action for you to take in MOST cases is to

    A. encourage full but orderly participation by all the men
    B. end the meeting and issue a bulletin instead
    C. tell them to hold their comments and questions until after you have finished
    D. tell those who interrupt that they are being unfair to the others

45. When one of your subordinates takes unusually long lunch hours, you tell him that this practice must stop.
Of the following, the BEST reason for speaking to him about this is that

    A. he will take even longer lunch hours unless you speak to him
    B. morale of your other subordinates may be impaired unless the situation is corrected
    C. work cannot be done in time unless the practice is discontinued
    D. your other subordinates will take the same amount of time for lunch as he does

46. You have just been assigned a new employee who has had a college education but has had no experience in stock work. Of the following, the BEST course of action for you to take is to

    A. attempt to have him transferred as soon as possible
    B. explain to him that he probably would not like the work
    C. make special efforts to ease his relationships with the other workers
    D. treat him the same as you would treat any other new worker

47. The morale of your subordinates seems unusually high. They tell you that it is because they have heard that one of them is to get a provisional promotion. You know definitely that this is not true.
   The MOST advisable action for you to take is to

   A. act as if you are happy to hear the good news
   B. let the situation take its normal course
   C. report the matter to your supervisor
   D. tell them that, so far as you know, the rumor is not justified

48. In most cases, the FIRST step to take in the event of serious injury in the storeroom is to

   A. search the employee for instructions pertaining to medical care
   B. send for medical help
   C. take the employee to a hospital
   D. treat the injury

49. An employee has accidentally cut his arm and is bleeding profusely.
   The one of the following which should NOT be done is to

   A. apply pressure above the injury
   B. give the employee a mild stimulant
   C. keep the employee at complete rest
   D. raise the bleeding part

50. When gasoline and all other highly inflammable substances are stored outdoors, the *No Smoking* rule should be

   A. observed for indoor and outdoor storage areas
   B. observed for indoor storage areas only
   C. observed for outdoor storage areas only
   D. eliminated for indoor and outdoor storage areas

KEY (CORRECT ANSWERS)

1. D	11. C	21. B	31. A	41. B
2. A	12. A	22. B	32. C	42. D
3. A	13. C	23. D	33. C	43. C
4. D	14. B	24. C	34. D	44. A
5. C	15. B	25. B	35. B	45. B
6. B	16. B	26. C	36. D	46. D
7. D	17. A	27. B	37. A	47. D
8. C	18. C	28. D	38. C	48. B
9. A	19. A	29. B	39. C	49. B
10. A	20. A	30. D	40. D	50. A

EXAMINATION SECTION
TEST 1

DIRECTIONS: Each question or incomplete statement is followed by several suggested answers or completions. Select the one that BEST answers the question or completes the statement. *PRINT THE LETTER OF THE CORRECT ANSWER IN THE SPACE AT THE RIGHT.*

1. For the GREATEST economy in transporting stock, one should 1.____

    A. divide the load into as many easily managed units as possible
    B. replace machines with men whenever possible
    C. transport as large a load as possible at one time
    D. utilize conveyor belts for most transporting

2. Assume that a new piece of equipment has been devised that would cut the labor cost of a certain major operation 75% and the time 50%. The monetary savings to the city would be such that the machine would pay for itself in one year. However, the old equipment is still in good working condition.
The MOST advisable recommendation to make is that the 2.____

    A. *new* equipment be purchased
    B. *new* equipment be purchased only if the old equipment can be sold at a reasonable price
    C. *new* equipment be rented
    D. *old* equipment be retained until there is moderate deterioration

3. Economy in handling stock can be measured BEST in terms of the 3.____

    A. cost of the equipment used
    B. cost of stock-handling operations
    C. overhead cost plus depreciation of equipment
    D. salaries being paid to the men

4. It is MOST economical and efficient to have good lighting available in 4.____

    A. all parts of the storehouse
    B. packing areas only
    C. receiving areas only
    D. storage areas only

5. If a great deal of heavy work must be completed by men under your supervision, it is MOST advisable, when possible, to 5.____

    A. give frequent rest periods
    B. have the men work overtime
    C. have the men listen to lively music while working
    D. shorten the lunch hour

6. A storehouse USUALLY operates at GREATEST efficiency when it stores _____ stock than it is designed to hold. 6.____

    A. slightly less
    B. slightly more
    C. substantially more
    D. the exact amount of

49

7. Usually, a report should be prepared with AT LEAST

   A. one copy so that there is a copy for future reference
   B. two copies so that the report can be sent to more than one person
   C. two copies so that there is an extra copy for your supervisor
   D. three copies so that there will be sufficient copies if they are needed

8. Of the following, the one which can MOST easily be increased or improved in an employee by his foreman or supervisor is

   A. ability to learn
   B. aptitude
   C. common sense
   D. knowledge

9. Two men under your supervision who are required to work together are not able to get along with each other. You have attempted to remedy this situation but without any success. One is an older man who has been in the section for many years, and the other is a recently-appointed younger man. Both men are capable employees.
   Of the following, the MOST advisable course of action for you to take is to recommend that the

   A. older man be transferred
   B. two men be given below-average service ratings
   C. younger man be discharged at the end of his probationary period
   D. younger man be transferred

10. Inefficient scheduling of work should be suspected when one notes that there are several men

    A. absent from work
    B. in the rest room
    C. loading a truck
    D. waiting to use equipment

11. *It is better to haul than to carry.*
    The PRIMARY reason for this statement is that

    A. stock should not be placed on top of any movable equipment
    B. stockmen should not be allowed to carry stock for any great distance
    C. the same power can usually pull more than it can carry
    D. there is less danger of damage when stock is hauled

12. After you have given a newly-appointed subordinate complete instructions on how to use a handtruck, you should usually

    A. assign him to work with another subordinate
    B. go over the instructions once more
    C. let him use the handtruck while you watch him
    D. tell him about the importance of the work

13. One of your subordinates tells you that he wants to submit a suggestion to the suggestion program regarding the operation of the storeroom but that he wants your advice first. The MOST advisable course of action for you to take is to

    A. advise him that any suggestions concerning the storeroom should be made directly to you
    B. give him advice provided he includes your name on the suggestion

C. give him the advice he needs
D. tell him that it would not be fair if you were to give him any help

14. Assume that you are in charge of one section of a storehouse. When the man in charge of an adjoining section resigns, you are asked to assume that job in addition to your own. After several weeks, you find that it is impossible for you to provide adequate supervision for both sections.
Of the following, the BEST course of action for you to take is to

    A. ask your supervisor for a transfer
    B. assign one subordinate in each section the job of supervision
    C. divide your time between the two sections
    D. inform your supervisor of the facts

15. Your subordinates tell you that, in your absence, your supervisor gave them orders which differed from those which you had given them.
In this case, you should

    A. discuss the matter with your subordinates to determine which orders are correct
    B. discuss the matter with your supervisor
    C. tell your subordinates to follow your orders
    D. tell your subordinates to follow your supervisor's orders

16. Assume that one of your subordinates made an error in recording an issue of stock. The mistake was found and corrected, but your subordinate seems rather depressed about the matter.
Of the following, the MOST advisable course of action for you to take is to

    A. ignore the entire situation unless it happens again
    B. praise him
    C. reprimand him mildly
    D. show him how he can avoid such a mistake in the future

17. Assume that you have the following equipment available: two forklift trucks, one tractor, six trailers, and four handtrucks.
In order to move twenty pallet loads 200 yards in a storehouse, it would be MOST advisable for you to use the

    A. forklift trucks
    B. forklift trucks, the tractor, and the trailers
    C. handtrucks, the tractor, and the trailers
    D. tractor and the trailers

18. Small cartons to be stored for a period of a year would usually be BEST stored on

    A. dollies   B. pallets   C. the floor   D. trailers

19. The one of the following types of equipment which should generally be used to collect a small number of items from various parts of the storehouse for a single shipment is a

    A. four-wheel truck   B. pallet
    C. skid   D. two-wheel truck

20. In a large city storehouse, main aisles used for movement of materials should usually be NOT less than _____ ft.

   A. 1　　　B. 2　　　C. 4　　　D. 6

21. An aisle used only as a fire aisle should be APPROXIMATELY _____ feet wide.

   A. 2　　　B. 5　　　C. 8　　　D. 10

22. When a perishable commodity is received at the storeroom, the factor which is generally LEAST important to consider when deciding where to store it is the

   A. activity of the commodity
   B. size and weight of the commodity
   C. temperature and humidity of the storage areas
   D. total storage capacity of the storeroom

23. Ten cartons of a certain item are stacked on each of ten pallets standing in a row. Assume that the men and equipment mentioned below are available.
   In order to move the cartons, with or without the pallets, from their place in the storehouse into a waiting truck, a distance of 25 yards, it would be MOST efficient to

   A. form a line of men to pass the cartons into the truck
   B. have a forklift truck take each pallet load separately and load it on the truck
   C. have one man move each pallet load with a hand lift pallet truck
   D. transfer the cartons from the pallets to a single tractor trailer train and then load them on the truck

24. The one of the following circumstances in which it would be MOST appropriate to use a fixed-platform power truck rather than a forklift truck is when

   A. loading a railroad car
   B. miscellaneous small items must be selected for a single shipment
   C. the load must be carried over a long distance
   D. there is a shortage of manpower

25. Storing small items in their original containers is a

   A. *bad* practice because it encourages laziness
   B. *bad* practice because it is disorderly
   C. *good* practice because it decreases handling
   D. *good* practice because it eliminates the need for shelves and bins

KEY (CORRECT ANSWERS)

1. C
2. A
3. B
4. A
5. A

6. D
7. A
8. D
9. D
10. D

11. C
12. C
13. C
14. D
15. B

16. D
17. B
18. B
19. A
20. D

21. A
22. D
23. B
24. B
25. C

TEST 2

DIRECTIONS: Each question or incomplete statement is followed by several suggested answers or completions. Select the one that BEST answers the question or completes the statement. *PRINT THE LETTER OF THE CORRECT ANSWER IN THE SPACE AT THE RIGHT.*

1. Assume that you have to move two cartons to a location about 50 feet away. Each carton weighs 10 pounds and measures 2' x 4' x 4'.
   Of the following, the method of moving the cartons which would ordinarily be BEST is to

   A. have two men carry each carton
   B. make one trip using a two-wheel handtruck
   C. make two trips using a two-wheel handtruck
   D. put both cartons on a four-wheel handtruck

2. Assume that you have to move two cartons to a location about 25 feet away. Each carton weighs 10 pounds and measures 6" x 12" x 18".
   Of the following, the method of moving the cartons which would ordinarily be BEST is to

   A. have one man carry both cartons in one trip
   B. have one man make two trips
   C. put both cartons on a four-wheel handtruck
   D. put both cartons on a two-wheel handtruck

3. Assume that you have to move twenty 10-pound cartons to a location about 100 feet away.
   Of the following, the method of moving the cartons which would ordinarily be BEST is to

   A. get a team of men to carry them by hand
   B. load them on a pallet and use a forklift truck
   C. load them on a skid and push the skid
   D. make a line of men and pass them from hand to hand

4. Assume that you have to move fifty pallets from one location in the warehouse to another about 250 feet away. Of the following, the equipment that you would need to do the job MOST efficiently is

   A. forklift truck, tractor, trailers
   B. four-wheel handtruck, portable elevator
   C. two-wheel handtruck, tractor, trailers
   D. two-wheel handtruck, trailers

5. The principle of *first-in, first-out* should generally be applied

   A. only to commodities subject to deterioration
   B. only to dated commodities
   C. only to perishable commodities
   D. to most commodities

6. A worker who is lifting a heavy object from the floor to a shoulder height position should preferably

   A. bend his knees, keep his back straight, and jerk the object to shoulder height in one quick motion
   B. bend his knees, keep his back straight, and lift to shoulder height in a slow continuous motion
   C. lift the object waist high, rest one end of it on a ledge, and then, while bending the knees, raise it to shoulder height
   D. lift the object waist high, rest one end of it on a ledge, and then, while keeping the knees straight, raise it to shoulder height

7. You have in stock a full drum of liquid which is lying on its side. You assign two men to stand it upright.
   The proper position for the men to take is for _____ to stand _____ of the drum.

   A. both; at the bottom end   B. both; at the top end
   C. each; on opposite ends   D. each; on opposite sides

8. Assume that you are employed in a well organized storehouse. Your stock records indicate that 450 units of a certain commodity are in stock. You count these items on a shelf and find only 175.
   The MOST advisable action for you to take FIRST is to

   A. consult the locator system
   B. count these items again
   C. recompute the stock balance
   D. report the shortage

9. A certain item is stored in a number of locations throughout a storeroom. You have counted the items in each location and added the numbers to get the total.
   Of the following, the BEST way to make sure that your figures are correct is to

   A. add the numbers again, using a different method
   B. add the numbers again, using the same method
   C. count the items again and recompute
   D. move all the items to one location

10. In taking inventory, you count much more of a certain item than is shown on the inventory card.
    Of the following, the MOST advisable action for you to take FIRST is to

    A. put an adjusting entry on the inventory card
    B. refer the matter to your supervisor
    C. review all requisitions since the last inventory record
    D. recheck the figures on the card

11. Assume that paper is issued at the rate of 500 reams per month. Three-hole punches are issued at the rate of 1 a month.
Of the following alternatives, it would probably be MOST practical and economic to order

    A. 500 reams per month and one three-hole punch per month
    B. 1,500 reams four times a year and 12 three-hole punches once a year
    C. 2,000 reams three times a year and 60 three-hole punches once every 5 years
    D. 18,000 reams once every 3 years and 36 three-hole punches once every 3 years

12. Assume that the price of an item is much lower during the months of June, July, and August However, you issue it throughout the year at the rate of 100 per month. The delivery time is one month, and you keep a one-month's reserve on hand at all times. You have enough room for 600 items.
Of the following, it would ordinarily be BEST for you to order

    A. 200 in June, 500 in August, and 500 in January
    B. 400 in June, 400 in August, and 400 in December
    C. 600 in July and 600 in December
    D. 500 in June, 200 in July, and 500 in August

13. Assume that one of the items which you stock is issued only during April, May, and June at the rate of 400 per month. You keep a one-month's supply on hand at all times, although you have sufficient room for an unlimited supply. The delivery time is one month.
Assuming that there are sufficient funds available at all times, it would probably be BEST for you to order

    A. 100 each month of the year
    B. 400 in March, 400 in April, and 400 in May
    C. 400 in April, 400 in May, and 400 in June
    D. 1,200 in March

14. Assume that you stock an item which deteriorates rapidly after 2 months. This item is issued at an average rate of 100 per month. The delivery time is one month. You keep a reserve supply of 20.
If these figures are maintained, you should order _____ iteris once _____ month(s).

    A. 100; a   B. 200; every two
    C. 220; every two   D. 300; every three

15. Assume that you have 50 boxes of a particular item on hand. The minimum order point is 100, and you have already ordered 300 boxes, which is the usual 3-months' supply. This order has not yet been delivered, and you have just received a special requisition for an additional 300 boxes.
Of the following, the MOST advisable action for you to take is to order

    A. 300 boxes immediately
    B. 300 boxes as soon as your outstanding order has been received
    C. 600 boxes immediately
    D. 600 boxes at the end of the present 3-month period

16. When a new model of a certain item is manufactured, you still have in stock a number of items of the old model. The old model is usable, but all the requisitions call for the new model.
Asking the requesting agencies or individuals to accept the old model instead is

16._____

   A. *desirable* because the best items should be issued last
   B. *desirable* because you will not be left with obsolete stock
   C. *undesirable* because it is interfering with their prerogatives
   D. *undesirable* because they should not be penalized for your errors

17. You are planning to submit an initial order for a new item. You estimate that you will issue 10 per month, and you want to have a one month's supply in reserve. You will reorder this item every three months.
Your initial order should be for

17._____

   A. 10 B. 20 C. 30 D. 40

18. You have room in the storehouse for 1,000 cartons of a certain item. Assume that you issue 100 boxes per month and always keep a one-month's supply in reserve. You order supplies every six months. Delivery time is thirty days.
Of the following, the MOST appropriate amount to order under usual circumstances is

18._____

   A. 500 B. 600 C. 700 D. 1,000

19. The PRINCIPAL disadvantage of having an order-picker fill two or more orders at one time is that

19._____

   A. more equipment is needed
   B. the order-picker will resent the burden
   C. the work must be scheduled more precisely
   D. there is greater chance of error

20. Of the following, the MOST important reason for having a physical inventory as well as a perpetual inventory is that a physical inventory

20._____

   A. enables a physical inspection of the items to determine their condition
   B. familiarizes the men with the stock
   C. gives a count of the number of items actually on hand
   D. provides an opportunity to clean up the area

21. Of the following conditions, the one which is properly represented by an annual stock turnover of 2.0 is _____ original stock has been replaced _____.

21._____

   A. half of the; during the year
   B. the; once during the year
   C. the; twice during the year
   D. the; once every two months

22. Of the following kinds of items, the one for which frequent inspections are MOST necessary is the item which is

22._____

   A. dated B. heavy C. plastic D. small

23. Of the following items, the one for which physical counts should be made MOST frequently is

   A. nails B. pipes C. valves D. wrenches

24. In order to avoid any interruption in normal storehouse operations during physical inventory, it would be necessary to

   A. close each section as it is inventoried
   B. close the storehouse during inventory
   C. inventory only on alternate days
   D. inventory after working hours or on weekends

25. It would be desirable to reduce stock levels to a one month period when the item is

   A. *expensive* and can be readily obtained
   B. *expensive* and difficult to obtain
   C. *inexpensive* and can be readily obtained
   D. *inexpensive* and difficult to obtain

KEY (CORRECT ANSWERS)

1.	D	11.	B
2.	A	12.	B
3.	B	13.	D
4.	A	14.	A
5.	D	15.	A
6.	C	16.	B
7.	D	17.	D
8.	A	18.	B
9.	C	19.	D
10.	D	20.	C

21.	C
22.	A
23.	D
24.	D
25.	A

EXAMINATION SECTION
TEST 1

DIRECTIONS: Each question or incomplete statement is followed by several suggested answers or completions. Select the one that BEST answers the question or completes the statement. *PRINT THE LETTER OF THE CORRECT ANSWER IN THE SPACE AT THE RIGHT.*

1. One of the results of understocking is that

   A. more money is tied up in stock
   B. stock must be ordered more frequently
   C. there is greater likelihood of obsolescence
   D. there is uneven distribution of materials in storage

2. Assume that your re-order point is obtained by multiplying the monthly rate of consumption by the lead time (in months) and adding the minimum balance. For a particular item, the re-order point is established at 200 units.
   If the lead time is 2 months and the minimum balance is 100, then the average monthly rate of consumption is

   A. 50   B. 100   C. 150   D. 200

3. If a certain item has shown no activity for two years, the MOST advisable action to take FIRST is to

   A. attempt to dispose of the item through salvage
   B. contact the using agencies or individuals to determine whether they can use the item
   C. contact the vendor to determine whether the item can be traded in
   D. write it off on the inventory control card

4. The MOST important information on an inventory control card is that which gives the _____ of the item.

   A. identity   B. location
   C. rate of consumption   D. vendor

5. A space 5 1/4 feet wide and 2 1/3 feet long has an area measuring MOST NEARLY _____ square feet.

   A. 9   B. 10   C. 11   D. 12

6. One man is able to load two 2 1/2-ton trucks in one hour. To load ten such trucks, it will take ten men _____ hour(s).

   A. 1/2   B. 1   C. 2   D. 2 1/2

7. If the average height of the stacks in your section of the storehouse is 10 feet, the area which will be occupied by 56,000 cubic feet of supplies is MOST likely to be

   A. 70' x 80'   B. 60' x 90'   C. 50' x 60'   D. 560' x 100'

8. The number of cartons, each measuring two cubic feet, which can fit into a space which is 100 square feet in area and is 8 feet high is MOST NEARLY

   A. 50 B. 200 C. 400 D. 800

9. When the floor area measures 200 feet by 200 feet and the maximum weight it can hold is 4,000 tons, then the safe floor load is _____ pounds per square foot.

   A. 20 B. 160 C. 200 D. 400

10. A carton 1' x 1' x 3' measures _____ cubic yards.

    A. 1/3 B. 1/9 C. 3 D. 9

11. You have received six cartons, each containing sixty boxes of staples, priced at $36.00 per carton.
    The price per box is

    A. $.10 B. $.60 C. $3.60 D. $6.00

12. The amount of space, in cubic feet, required to store 100 boxes each measuring 24" x 12" x 6" is MOST NEARLY

    A. 10 B. 100 C. 168 D. 1008

13. Assume that it takes an average of two man-hours to stack 1 ton of certain supplies. In order to stack 30 tons, the number of men required to complete the job in ten hours is

    A. 6 B. 10 C. 15 D. 30

14. An area measures 20 feet by 22 1/2 feet. The floor load is 100 pounds per square foot. The total weight that can be stored in this area is MOST NEARLY _____ pounds.

    A. 450 B. 9,000 C. 22,500 D. 45,000

15. The price of a certain type of linoleum is $.20 per square foot.
    The total cost of four pieces of 9' x 12' linoleum is MOST NEARLY

    A. $21 B. $80 C. $86 D. $432

16. The number of board feet in a piece of lumber measuring 2 inches thick by 2 feet wide by 12 feet long is

    A. 12 B. 16 C. 24 D. 48

17. If 39 3/8 ounces of a certain commodity are on hand and two requisitions are filled, one for 9 1/2 and one for 9 5/6 ounces, the number of ounces remaining are

    A. 18 2/3 B. 19 1/3 C. 20 1/24 D. 20 3/4

18. In order to fill 96 bottles containing 3 fluid ounces each, the number of pints which would be needed is

    A. 9 B. 18 C. 32 D. 36

19. If a section of a storeroom measures 29 feet 4 inches by 18 feet 3 inches, the total area is MOST NEARLY _____ square feet.

    A. 523 B. 524 C. 535 D. 537

20. A discount of 1% is given on all purchases of over 100 brushes. An additional discount of 1% is given on all purchases of over 500 brushes.
    If 600 brushes are purchased at a list price of $2.07 each, the total cost is MOST NEARLY

    A. $1217   B. $1228   C. $1230   D. $2484

21. The following items are purchased: 30 locksets at $15.00 per dozen, and 10 gross of stove bolts at 1 1/2 cents each bolt.
    The total cost is MOST NEARLY

    A. $60   B. $180   C. $255   D. $470

22. The cost of one dozen pieces of screening, each measuring 4'6" by 5', at $.10 per square foot, is

    A. $22.50   B. $25.00   C. $27.00   D. $27.60

23. The amount of turpentine on hand is 39 gallons. One requisition is filled for 3 1/2 gallons, three additional requisitions are filled for 3 quarts each, and six requisitions are filled for 1 pint each.
    The quantity of turpentine remaining after all these requisitions have been filled is

    A. 32 gal.   B. 32 gal. 1 qt.
    C. 32 gal. 2 qts.   D. 32 gal. 3 qts.

24. A shelf is 30" wide and 20" deep. The shelf is filled solid with 500 boxes, each measuring 2" x 3" x 5". The distance from the shelf to the top of the stacked boxes is

    A. 10"   B. 25"   C. 50"   D. 60"

25. In order to check on a shipment of 1000 articles, a sampling of 100 articles was carefully inspected.
    Of the sample, one article was wholly defective and 4 more were partly defective.
    On this basis, the percentage of completely acceptable articles in the original shipment is probably MOST NEARLY

    A. 5%   B. 10%   C. 95%   D. 100%

26. The one of the following which is NOT the name of a type of screwdriver is

    A. cabinet   B. flat-nose
    C. knife handle   D. spiral ratchet

27. Pupil Dental Record forms are likely to be used in GREATEST quantities by the

    A. Board of Education   B. Department of Health
    C. Department of Hospitals   D. Department of Social Service

28. Crepe paper is likely to be requisitioned MOST frequently by the

    A. Board of Education   B. Department of Public Events
    C. Housing Authority   D. Transit Authority

29. Scalpels are likely to be requisitioned MOST frequently by the Department of

   A. Correction B. Health
   C. Hospitals D. Parks

30. Pruners are likely to be requisitioned MOST frequently by the

   A. Department of Parks B. Department of Sanitation
   C. Reference Library D. Transit Authority

31. Fustats are likely to be requisitioned MOST frequently by the

   A. Department of Markets B. Fire Department
   C. Housing Authority D. Police Department

32. Machine screws are usually purchased in large quantities by the

   A. bushel B. gross C. pound D. score

33. A No. 10 can of fruit juice contains about

   A. eight ounces B. one pint
   C. one quart D. three quarts

34. Sulphuric acid is USUALLY purchased in large quantities by the

   A. carboy B. drum C. gallon D. cylinder

35. The one of the following which is NOT a standard size of index card is

   A. 3x5 B. 4x6 C. 5 x 7 D. 5 x 8

36. The label on a package of mimeograph paper reads: Size 8 1/2 x 11, Basis 20. *Basis 20* refers to the

   A. color code for this type of paper
   B. quality and finish of the paper
   C. way in which the paper is packaged
   D. weight of the paper

37. You tell a man to separate and store cans of paint in a certain way. The man then asks you, *Why do you want me to do it this way?*
   You should answer his question by

   A. advising him to figure out the reason himself
   B. explaining to him why you want it done in that particular way
   C. repeating your instructions more slowly
   D. telling him to follow your instructions without asking any questions

38. Assume that an employee shows you that you have made an error in issuing certain instructions. You admit your error.
   Such action on your part is desirable PRIMARILY because

   A. the job may be done correctly
   B. your men will be encouraged to make similar corrections in the future
   C. you will gain a reputation for fairness
   D. your men will realize that you will not make errors of this type in the future

39. Assume that you have just been promoted. Your supervisor gives you detailed oral instructions as to how a particular category of stock should be stored. At the conclusion of his instructions, you realize that you do not fully understand how your supervisor wishes to have the stock stored.
Under these circumstances, you should

    A. ask an experienced worker to clarify your supervisor's instructions
    B. ask your supervisor to clarify anything that you do not understand
    C. ask your supervisor to put his instructions in writing
    D. carry out your supervisor's instructions as best as you can

40. You have reason to believe that one of your men is taking merchandise which does not belong to him from the storehouse. You question the man about this. He tells you that he borrowed the merchandise and intends to return it. Under these Circumstances, you should probably

    A. disregard the matter until such time as you have evidence which will stand up in court
    B. offer to accompany the man to his home to pick up the property in question
    C. report the matter to your supervisor
    D. tell the man to return the property as soon as he has finished using it

41. A truck which must be unloaded immediately arrives at the storehouse. You issue instructions to your crew as to how this should be done. One of your men strongly objects and says that your instructions are wrong. You listen to his reasons but you still think that you are right. Under these circumstances, you should

    A. ask for opinions from the other men in the crew as to how the job should be done
    B. contact another worker to get his opinion
    C. refer the matter to your supervisor for his decision
    D. tell the men to unload the truck in accordance with your instructions

42. Whenever you give an assignment to one of your experienced men, he asks you a great many questions about it although he has successfully performed similar assignments in the past. The time you spend in answering his many questions about minor details takes you away from more important work.
Under these circumstances, you should probably FIRST

    A. answer his questions in such a way that he will be discouraged from asking further questions
    B. ask the man to ask his questions of one of his fellow employees
    C. assure the man of your confidence in his ability to carry out the assignment
    D. tell the man that if the assignment is too difficult you will give it to someone who does not raise so many questions

43. You have reason to believe that one of the men in your crew gossips about you behind your back.
Under these circumstances, it is usually BEST to

    A. attempt to find out which of your men believes the gossip
    B. find out what the man's weak points are and bring them to the attention of your crew

C. ignore the matter
D. speak to the man about it and tell him to stop

44. Your supervisor gives you an assignment which you believe you cannot do since you do not have a sufficient number of men. You explain this to your supervisor but he tells you to get the job done.
You should

   A. do the best you can and keep your supervisor informed of the progress you are making
   B. report the matter to your main office
   C. insist that your supervisor give you his instructions in writing
   D. wait until your supervisor gives you more men before taking any action to carry out the assignment

45. Your crew consistently performs more work than the crew headed by another worker. The other worker tells you that the high performance of your crew makes his crew *look bad*.
Under these circumstances, it would be BEST for you to

   A. ignore the matter and have your crew continue working as before
   B. report the matter to your supervisor for disciplinary action
   C. slow your crew down somewhat to show the other man that you are willing to cooperate with him
   D. slow your crew down to the level of the other crew

46. Two of your men frequently argue with each other so that the work of your crew is disrupted.
You should FIRST

   A. attempt to find out why the men argue with each other
   B. speak to the two men privately regarding their possible transfer to another crew
   C. submit a report to your supervisor setting forth the facts
   D. tell both men that unless they stop arguing you will see that they are given below-standard service ratings

47. One of your men asks you to put him in for an above-standard service rating. His work has been good but it has not been above-standard.
You should tell the man that

   A. he has done good work but that in your judgment his work has not been above-standard
   B. if you recommend him for an above-standard service rating, you will have to do the same thing for most of the others in your crew
   C. you cannot discuss the matter with him but that you will discuss it with your supervisor
   D. you will speak to the other men in the crew and if no one objects you will recommend him for a higher service rating

48. You receive a memorandum from your supervisor in which he instructs you to make a large number of changes in the procedures for storing materials.
    The BEST way to bring these changes to the attention of your crew is to

    A. post the memorandum on the bulletin board where everyone can read it
    B. meet individually with each member of your staff to discuss the changes
    C. hold a meeting with your crew and explain the changes to them
    D. see to it that the memorandum is circulated to and initialled by each member of the crew

49. Although you have frequently spoken to one of your men regarding the proper way of lifting heavy objects, he persists in ignoring your instructions. He says that he knows the proper way of lifting, that you do not, and that he does not intend to hurt himself by following your instructions.
    Of the following, the BEST course of action for you to take is to

    A. assign the man to tasks which do not involve heavy lifting
    B. ignore the matter as long as the man does not hurt himself
    C. put your instructions on how to lift in writing and give a copy of your instructions to each man in the crew
    D. report the matter to your supervisor

50. You assign a man to take inventory of a certain item. The man gives you a figure which seems too high. Of the following, the BEST course of action for you to take is to

    A. accept the figure given to you by the man if he is willing to initial it
    B. accompany the man while he takes inventory again
    C. ask the man to take inventory again and tell him why
    D. take inventory yourself

KEY (CORRECT ANSWERS)

1. B	11. B	21. A	31. C	41. D
2. A	12. B	22. C	32. B	42. C
3. B	13. A	23. C	33. D	43. C
4. A	14. D	24. B	34. A	44. A
5. D	15. C	25. C	35. C	45. A
6. A	16. D	26. B	36. D	46. A
7. A	17. C	27. A	37. B	47. A
8. C	18. B	28. A	38. A	48. C
9. C	19. C	29. C	39. B	49. D
10. B	20. A	30. A	40. C	50. C

EXAMINATION SECTION
TEST 1

DIRECTIONS: Each question or incomplete statement is followed by several suggested answers or completions. Select the one that BEST answers the question or completes the statement. *PRINT THE LETTER OF THE CORRECT ANSWER IN THE SPACE AT THE RIGHT.*

1. A supervisor was given a booklet that showed a new work method that could save time. He didn't tell his men because he thought that they would get the booklet anyway.
   For the supervisor to have acted like this is a
   A. *good* idea, because he saves time and both of talking to the men
   B. *bad* idea, because he should make sure his men know about better work methods
   C. *good* idea, because the men would rather read about it themselves
   D. *bad* idea, because a supervisor should always show his men every memo he gets from higher authority

1.____

2. A supervisor found it necessary to discipline two subordinates. One man had been operating his equipment in a wrong way, while the other man came to work late for three days in a row. The supervisor decided to talk to both men together.
   For the supervisor to deal with the problems in this way is a
   A. *good* idea because each man will learn about the difficulties of the other person and how to solve such difficulties
   B. *bad* idea because the supervisor should wait until he can bring a larger group together and save time in discussing such questions
   C. *good* idea because he will be able to get the men to see that their problems are related
   D. *bad* idea because he should meet with each man separately and give him his full attention

2.____

3. A supervisor should try to make his men feel their jobs are important in order to
   A. get the men to say good things about their supervisor to his own superior
   B. get the men to think in terms of advancing to better jobs
   C. let higher management in the agency know that the supervisor is efficient
   D. help the men to be able to work more efficiently and enthusiastically

3.____

4. A supervisor should know approximately how long it takes to do a particular kind of job CHIEFLY because he
   A. will know how much time to take if he has to do it himself
   B. will be able to tell his men to do it even faster
   C. can judge the performance of the person doing the job
   D. can retrain experienced employees in better work habits

4.____

5. Supervisors often get their employees' opinions about better work methods because
   A. the men will know that they are respected
   B. the men would otherwise lose all their confidence in the supervisor
   C. the supervisor might find in this way a good suggestion he could use
   D. this is the best method for improvement of work methods

6. Right after you have trained your subordinates in doing a new job, you find that they seem to be doing all right, but that it will take them several days to finish. You also have several groups of men working at other locations.
   The MOST efficient way for you to make sure that the men continue doing the new job properly is to
   A. stay on that job with the men until it is finished just in case trouble develops
   B. visit the men every half hour until the job is done
   C. stay away from their job that day and visit the men the next day to ask them if they had any problems
   D. visit the men a few times each day until they finish the new job

7. Assume that one of your new employees is older than you are. You also think that he may be hard to get along with because he is older than you.
   The BEST way for you to avoid any problems with the older worker is for you to
   A. lay down the law immediately and tell the man he better not cause you any trouble
   B. treat the man just the way you would any other worker
   C. always ask the older worker for advice in the presence of all the men
   D. ignore the man entirely until he realizes that you are the boss

8. Assume that you have tried a new method suggested by one of your employees and find that it is easier and cheaper than the method you had been using.
   The PROPER thing for you to do NEXT is to
   A. say nothing to anyone but train your men to use the new method
   B. train your men to use the new method and tell your crew that you got the idea from one of the men
   C. continue using the old method because a supervisor should not use suggestions of his men
   D. have your crew learn the new method and take credit for the idea since you are the boss

9. Suppose you are a supervisor and your superior tells you that the way your men are doing a certain procedure is wrong and that you should re-train our men as soon as possible.
   When you begin to re-train the men, the FIRST thing you should do is to
   A. tell your men that a wrong procedure had been used and that a new method must be learned as a result
   B. train your employees in the new method with no explanation since you are the boss

C. tell the crew that your superior has just decided that everyone should learn a new method
D. tell the crew that your superior says your method is wrong but that you don't agree with this

10. It is BAD practice to criticize a man in front of the other men because
    A. people will think you are too strict
    B. it is annoying to anyone who walks by
    C. it is embarrassing to the man concerned
    D. it will antagonize the other men

10.____

11. A supervisor decides not to put his two best men on a work detail because he knows that they won't like it.
    For the supervisor to make the work assignment this way is a
    A. *good* idea because it is only fair to give your best men a break once in a while
    B. *bad* idea because you should treat all of your me fairly and not show favoritism
    C. *good* idea because you save the strength of these men for another job
    D. *bad* idea because more of the men should be exempted from the assignment

11.____

12. Suppose you are a supervisor and you find it inconvenient to obey an established procedure set by your agency. You think another procedure would be better.
    The BEST thing to do first about this procedure that you don't like is for you to
    A. obey the procedure even if you don't to and suggest your idea to your own supervisor
    B. disregard the procedure because a supervisor is supposed to have some privileges
    C. follow the procedure some of the time but ignore it when the men are not watching
    D. organize a group of other supervisors to get the procedure changed

12.____

13. A supervisor estimated that it would take his crew one workday per week to do a certain job each week. However, after a month he noticed that the job averaged two and a half days a week and this delayed other jobs that had to be done.
    The FIRST thing that the supervisor should do in this case is to
    A. call him men together and warn them that they will get a poor work evaluation if they do not work harder
    B. talk to each man personally, asking him to work harder on the job
    C. go back and study the maintenance job by himself to see if more men should be assigned to the job
    D. write his boss a report describing in detail how much time it is taking the men to do the job

13.____

14. An employee complains to you that some of the work assignments are too difficult to do alone.
    Which of the following is the BEST way for you to handle this complaint?
    A. Go with him to see exactly what he does and why he finds it so difficult
    B. Politely tell the man that he has to do the job or be brought up on charges
    C. Tell the man to send his complaint to the head of your agency
    D. Sympathize with the man and give him easier jobs

15. The BEST way for a supervisor to keep control of his work assignments is to
    A. ask the men to report to him immediately when their jobs are finished
    B. walk around the buildings once a week and get a first-hand view of what is being done
    C. keep his ears open for problems and complaints, but leave the men aloe to do the work
    D. write up a work schedule and check it periodically against the actual work done

16. A supervisor made a work schedule for his men. At the bottom of it, he wrote, *No changes or exceptions will be made in this schedule for any reason.*
    For the supervisor to have made this statement is
    A. *good*, because the men will respect the supervisor for his attitude
    B. *bad*, because there are emergencies and special situations that occur
    C. *good*, because each man will know exactly what is expected of him
    D. *bad*, because the men should expect that no changes will ever be made in the work schedule without written permission

17. Which one of the following would NOT be a result of a well-planned work schedule?
    The schedule
    A. makes efficient use of the time of the staff
    B. acts as a checklist for an important job that might be left out
    C. will give an idea of the work to a substitute supervisor
    D. shows at a glance who the best men are

18. A new piece of equipment you have ordered is delivered. You are familiar with it, but the men under you who will use it do not know the equipment.
    Of the following methods, which is the BEST to take in explaining to them how to operate this equipment?
    A. Ask the men to watch other crews using the equipment
    B. Show one reliable man how to operate the equipment and ask him to teach the other men
    C. Ask the men to read the instructions in the manual for the equipment
    D. Call the men together and show them how to operate the equipment

19. One supervisor assigns work to his men by calling his crew together each week and describing what has to be done that week. He then tells them to arrange individual assignments among themselves and to work as a team during the week.

This method of scheduling work is a
- A. *good* idea because this guarantees that the men will work together
- B. *bad* idea because responsibility for doing the job is poorly fixed
- C. *good* idea because the men will finish the job in less time, working together
- D. *bad* idea because the supervisor should always stay with his men

20. Suppose that an employee came to his supervisor with a problem concerning his assignment.
For the supervisor to listen to his problem is a
- A. *good* idea because a supervisor should always take time off to talk when one of his men wants to talk
- B. *bad* idea because the supervisor should not be bothered during the work day
- C. *good* idea because it is the job of the supervisor to deal with problems of job assignment
- D. *bad* idea because the employee could start annoying the supervisor with all sorts of problems

21. Suppose that on the previous afternoon you were looking for an experienced employee in order to give him an emergency job and he was missing from his job location. The next morning, he tells you that he got sick suddenly and had to go home, but could not tell you since you were not around. He has never done this before.
What should you do?
- A. Tell the man he is excused and that in such circumstances he did the wisest thing
- B. Bring the man up on charges because whatever he says he could still have notified you
- C. Have the man examined by a doctor to see if he really was sick the day before
- D. Explain to the mean that he should make every effort to tell you or to get a message to you if he must leave

22. An employee had a grievance and went to his supervisor about it. The employee was not satisfied with the way the supervisor tried to help him and told him so. Yet, the supervisor had done everything he could under the circumstances.
The PROPER action for the supervisor to take at this time is to
- A. politely tell the employee that there is nothing more for the supervisor to do about the problem
- B. let the employee know how he can bring his complaint to a higher authority
- C. tell the employee that he must solve the problem on his own since he did not want to follow the supervisor's advice
- D. suggest to the employee that he ask for another supervisor for assistance

23. In which of the following situations is it BEST to give your men spoken rather than written orders?
    A. You want your men to have a record of the instructions.
    B. Spoken instructions are less likely to be forgotten.
    C. An emergency situation has arisen in which there is no time to write up instructions.
    D. There are instructions on time and leave regulations which are complicated.

24. One of your employees tells you that a week ago he had a small accident on the job but he did not bother telling you because he was able to continue working.
    For the employee not to have told his supervisor about the accident was
    A. *good*, because the accident was a small one
    B. *bad*, because all accidents should be reported, no matter how small
    C. *good*, because the supervisor should be bothered only for important matters
    D. *bad*, because having an accident is one way to get excused for the day

25. For a supervisor to deal with each of his subordinate in exactly the same manner is
    A. *poor*, because each man presents a different problem and there is no one way of handling all problems
    B. *good*, because once a problem is handled with one man, he can handle another man with the same problem
    C. *poor*, because the men will resent it if they are not handled each in a better way than others
    D. *good*, because this assures fair and impartial treatment of each subordinate

KEY (CORRECT ANSWERS)

1.	B	11.	B
2.	D	12.	A
3.	D	13.	C
4.	C	14.	A
5.	C	15.	D
6.	D	16.	B
7.	B	17.	D
8.	B	18.	D
9.	A	19.	B
10.	C	20.	C

21. D
22. B
23. C
24. B
25. A

TEST 2

DIRECTIONS: Each question or incomplete statement is followed by several suggested answers or completions. Select the one that BEST answers the question or completes the statement. *PRINT THE LETTER OF THE CORRECT ANSWER IN THE SPACE AT THE RIGHT.*

1. Jim Johnson has been on your staff for over four years. He has always been a conscientious and productive worker. About a month ago, his wife died; and since that time, his work performance has been very poor.
   As his supervisor, which one of the following is the BEST way for you to deal with this situation?
   A. Allow Jim as much time as he needs to overcome his grief and hope that his work performance improves
   B. Meet with Jim to discuss ways to improve his performance
   C. Tell Jim directly that you are more concerned with his work performance than with his personal problem
   D. Prepare disciplinary action on Jim as soon as possible

   1.____

2. You are responsible for the overall operation of a storehouse which is divided into two sections. Each section has its own supervisor. You have decided to make several complex changes in the storekeeping procedures which will affect both sections.
   Of the following, the BEST way to make sure that these changes are understood by the two supervisors is for you to
   A. meet with both supervisors to discuss the changes
   B. issue a memorandum to each supervisor explaining the changes
   C. post the changes where the supervisors are sure to see them
   D. instruct one supervisor to explain the changes to the other supervisor

   2.____

3. You have called a meeting of all your subordinates to tell them what has to be done on a new project in which they will all be involved. Several times during the meeting, you ask if there are any questions about what you have told them.
   Of the following, to ask the subordinates whether there are any questions during the meeting can BEST be described as
   A. *inadvisable*, because it interferes with their learning about the new project
   B. *advisable*, because you will find out what they don't understand and have a chance to clear up any problems they may have
   C. *inadvisable*, because it makes the meeting too long and causes the subordinates to lose interest in the new project
   D. *advisable*, because it gives you a chance to learn which of your subordinates are paying attention to what you say

   3.____

4. As a supervisor, you are responsible for seeing to it that absenteeism does not become a problem among your subordinates.
   Which one of the following is NOT an acceptable way of controlling the problem of excessive absences?

   4.____

A. Distribute a written statement to your staff on the policies regarding absenteeism in your organization
B. Arrange for workers who have the fewest absences to talk to those workers who have the most absences
C. Let your subordinates know that a record is being kept of all absences
D. Arrange for counseling of those employees who are frequently absent

5. One of your supervisors has been an excellent worker for the past two years. There are no promotion opportunities for this worker in the foreseeable future. Due to the city's present budget crisis, a salary increase is not possible.
Under the circumstances, which one of the following actions on your part would be MOST likely to continue to motivate this worker?
   A. Tell the worker that times are bad all over and jobs are hard to find
   B. Give the worker less work and easier assignments
   C. Tell the worker to try to look for a better paying job elsewhere
   D. Seek the worker's advice often and show that the suggestions provided are appreciated

5.____

6. As a supervisor in a warehouse, it is important that you use your available work force to its fullest potential.
Which one of the following actions on your part is MOST likely to increase the effectiveness of your work force?
   A. Assigning more workers to a job than the number actually needed
   B. Eliminating all job training to allow more time for work output
   C. Using your best workers on jobs that average workers can do
   D. Making sure that all materials and equipment used are maintained in good working order

6.____

7. You learn that your storage area will soon be undergoing changes which will affect the work of your subordinates. You decide not to tell your subordinates about what is to happen.
Of the following, your action can BEST be described as
   A. *wise*, because your subordinates will learn of the changes for themselves
   B. *unwise*, because your subordinates should be advised about what is to happen
   C. *wise*, because it is better for your subordinates to continue working without being disturbed by such news
   D. *unwise*, because the work of your subordinates will gradually slow down

7.____

8. In making plans for the operation of your unit, you are MOST likely to see these plans carried out successfully if you
   A. allow your staff to participate in developing these plans
   B. do not spend any time on the minor details of these plans
   C. base these plans on the past experiences of others
   D. allow these plans to interact with outside activities in other units

8.____

3 (#2)

9. As a supervisor in charge of the total operation of a food supply warehouse, you find vandalism to be a potentially serious problem. On occasion, trespassers have gained entrance into the facility by climbing over an unprotected 8-foot fence surrounding the warehouse whose dimensions measure 100 feet by 100 feet.
Assuming that all of the following would be equally effective ways in preventing these breaches in security in the situation described above, which one would be LEAST costly?
    A. Using two trained guard dogs to roam freely throughout the facility at night
    B. Hiring a security guard to patrol the facility after working hours
    C. Installing tape razor wire on top of the fence surrounding the facility
    D. Installing an electronic burglar alarm system requiring the installation of a new fence

9._____

10. The area for which you have program responsibility has undergone recent changes. Your staff is now required to perform many new tasks, and morale is low.
The LEAST effective way for you to improve long-term staff morale would be to
    A. develop support groups to discuss problems
    B. involve staff in job development
    C. maintain a comfortable social environment within the group
    D. adequately plan and give assignments in a timely manner

10._____

11. As a supervisor in a large office, one of your subordinate supervisors stops you in the middle of the office and complains loudly that he is being treated unfairly. The rest of the staff ceases work and listens to the complaint.
The MOST appropriate action for you to take in this situation is to
    A. ignore this unprofessional behavior and continue on your way
    B. tell the supervisor that his behavior is unprofessional and he should learn how to conduct himself
    C. explain to the supervisor why you believe he is not being treated unfairly
    D. ask the supervisor to come to your office at a specific time to discuss the matter

11._____

12. You are told that one of your subordinates is distributing literature which attempts to recruit individuals to join a particular organization. Several workers complain that their rights are being violated.
Of the following, the BEST action for you to take FIRST is to
    A. ignore the situation because no harm is being done
    B. discuss the matter further with your supervisor
    C. ask the worker to stop distributing the literature
    D. tell the workers that they do not have to read the material

12._____

13. You have been assigned to develop a short training course for a recently issued procedure.
In designing this course, which of the following statements is the LEAST important for you to consider?

13._____

A. The learning experience must be interesting and meaningful in terms of the staff member's job.
B. The method of teaching must be strictly followed in order to develop successful learning experiences.
C. The course content should incorporate the rules and regulations of the agency.
D. The procedure should be consistent with the agency's objectives.

14. As a supervisor, there are several newly-promoted employees under your supervision. Each of these employees is subject to a probationary period PRIMARILY to
    A. assess the employee's performance to see if the employee should be retained or removed from the position
    B. give the employee the option to return to his former employment if the employee is unhappy in the new position
    C. give the employee an opportunity to learn the duties and responsibilities of the position
    D. judge the employee's potential for upward mobility in the future

15. An employee under your supervision rushes into your office to tell you he has just received a telephone bomb threat.
    As the administrative supervisor, the FIRST thing you should do is
    A. evacuate staff from the floor
    B. call the police and building security
    C. advise your administrator
    D. do a preliminary search

16. After reviewing the Absence Control form for a unit under your supervision, you find that one of your staff members has a fifth undocumented sick leave within a six-month period.
    In this situation, the FIRST action you should take is to
    A. discuss the seriousness of the matter with the staff member when he returns to work and fully document the details of the discussion
    B. review the case with the location director and warn the staff member that future use of sick leave will be punished
    C. submit the proper disciplinary forms to ensure that the staff member is penalized for excessive absences
    D. request that the timekeeper put the staff member on doctor's note restriction

17. A subordinate supervisor recently assigned to your office begins his first conference with you by saying that he has learned something that another supervisor is doing that you should know about.
    After hearing this statement, of the following, the BEST approach for you to take is to
    A. explain to the supervisor that the conference is to discuss his work and not that of his co-workers
    B. tell the supervisor that you do not encourage a spy system among the staff you supervise

C. tell the supervisor that you will listen to his report only if the other supervisor is present
D. allow the supervisor to continue talking until you have enough information to make a decision on how best to respond

18. Assume that you are a supervisor recently assigned to a new unit. You notice that, for the past few days, one of the employees in your unit whose work is about average has been stopping work at about four o'clock and has been spending the rest of the afternoon relaxing at his desk.
The BEST of the following actions for you to take in this situation is to
   A. assign more work to this employee since it is apparent that he does not have enough work to keep him busy
   B. observe the employee's conduct more closely for about ten days before taking any more positive action
   C. discuss the matter with the employee, pointing out to him how he can use the extra hour daily to raise the level of his job performance
   D. question the previous supervisor in charge of the unit in order to determine whether he had sanctioned such conduct when he supervised that unit

18.____

19. A new supervisor was assigned to your program four months ago. Although he tries hard, he has been unable to meet certain standards because he still has a lot to learn. As his supervisor, you are required to submit performance evaluations within a few days.
How would you rate this employee on the tasks where he fails to meet standards because of lack of experience?
   A. Satisfactory   B. Conditional
   C. Unsatisfactory   D. Unratable

19.____

20. You find that there is an important procedural error in a memo which you distributed to your staff several days ago.
The BEST approach for you to take at this time is to
   A. send a corrected memo to the staff, indicating what prior error was made
   B. send a corrected memo to the staff without mentioning the prior error
   C. tell the staff about the error at the next monthly staff meeting
   D. place the corrected memo on the office bulletin board

20.____

21. Your superior asks you, a supervisor, about the status of the response to a letter from a public official concerning a client's case. When you ask the subordinate who was assigned to prepare the response to give you the letter, the subordinate denies that it was given to him. You are certain that the subordinate has the letter, but is withholding it because the response has not yet been prepared.
Of the following, in order to secure the letter from the subordinate, you should FIRST
   A. accuse the subordinate of lying and demand that the letter be given to you immediately
   B. say that you would consider it a personal favor if the subordinate would find the letter

21.____

C. continue to question the subordinate until he admits to having been given the letter
D. offer a face-saving solution, such as asking the subordinate to look again for the letter

22. As a supervisor, you have been assigned to write a few paragraphs to be included in the agency's annual report, describing a public service agency department this year as compared to last year.
Which of the following elements basic to the agency is LEAST likely to have changed since last year?
   A. Mission   B. Structure   C. Technology   D. Personnel

23. As a supervisor, you have been informed that a grievance has been filed against you, accusing you of assigning a subordinate to out-of-title tasks.
Of the following, the BEST approach for you to take is to
   A. waive the grievance so that it will proceed to a Step II hearing
   B. immediately change the subordinate's assignment to avoid future problems
   C. respond to the grievance, giving appropriate reasons for the assignment
   D. review the job description to ensure that the subordinate's tasks are not out-of-title

24. Which of the following is NOT a correct statement about agency group training programs in a public service agency?
   A. Training sessions continue for an indefinite period of time.
   B. Group training sessions are planned for designated personnel.
   C. Training groups are organized formally through administrative planning.
   D. Group training is task-centered and aimed toward accomplishing specific educational goals.

25. As a supervisor, you have submitted a memo to your superior requesting a conference to discuss the performance of a manager under your supervision. The memo states that the manager has a good working relationship with her staff; however, she tends to interpret agency policy too liberally and shows poor administrative skills by missing some deadlines and not keeping proper controls.
Which of the following steps should NOT be taken in order to prepare for this conference with your superior?
   A. Collect and review all your notes regarding the manager's prior performance.
   B. Outline your agenda so that you will have sufficient time to discuss the situation.
   C. Tell the manager that you will be discussing her performance with your superior.
   D. Clearly define objectives which will focus on improving the manager's performance.

KEY (CORRECT ANSWERS)

1.	B		11.	D
2.	A		12.	C
3.	B		13.	B
4.	B		14.	A
5.	D		15.	B
6.	D		16.	A
7.	B		17.	D
8.	A		18.	C
9.	C		19.	B
10.	C		20.	A

21. D
22. A
23. C
24. A
25. C

CLERICAL ABILITIES
EXAMINATION SECTION
TEST 1

DIRECTIONS: Each question or incomplete statement is followed by several suggested answers or completions. Select the one that BEST answers the question or completes the statement. *PRINT THE LETTER OF THE CORRECT ANSWER IN THE SPACE AT THE RIGHT.*

Questions 1-4.

DIRECTIONS: Questions 1 through 4 are to be answered on the basis of the information given below.

The most commonly used filing system and the one that is easiest to learn is alphabetical filing. This involves putting records in an A to Z order, according to the letters of the alphabet. The name of a person is filed by using the following order: first, the surname or last name; second, the first name; third, the middle name or middle initial. For example, *Henry C. Young* is filed under *Y* and thereafter under *Young, Henry C.* The name of a company is filed in the same way. For example, *Long Cabinet Co.* is filed under *L* while *John T. Long Cabinet Co.* is filed under *L* and thereafter under *Long, John T. Cabinet Co.*

1. The one of the following which lists the names of persons in the CORRECT alphabetical order is:
   A. Mary Carrie, Helen Carrol, James Carson, John Carter
   B. James Carson, Mary Carrie, John Carter, Helen Carrol
   C. Helen Carrol, James Carson, John Carter, Mary Carrie
   D. John Carter, Helen Carrol, Mary Carrie, James Carson

   1.____

2. The one of the following which lists the names of persons in the CORRECT alphabetical order is:
   A. Jones, John C.; Jones, John A.; Jones, John P.; Jones, John K.
   B. Jones, John P.; Jones, John K.; Jones, John C.; Jones, John A.
   C. Jones, John A.; Jones, John C.; Jones, John K.; Jones, John P.
   D. Jones, John K.; Jones, John C.; Jones, John A.; Jones, John P.

   2.____

3. The one of the following which lists the names of the companies in the CORRECT alphabetical order is:
   A. Blane Co., Blake Co., Block Co., Blear Co.
   B. Blake Co., Blane Co., Blear Co., Block Co.
   C. Block Co., Blear Co., Blane Co., Blake Co.
   D. Blear Co., Blake Co., Blane Co., Block Co.

   3.____

4. You are to return to the file an index card on *Barry C. Wayne Materials and Supplies Co.*
Of the following, the CORRECT alphabetical group that you should return the index card to is
   A. A to G   B. H to M   C. N to S   D. T to Z

4._____

Questions 5-10.

DIRECTIONS: In each of Questions 5 through 10, the names of four people are given. For each question, choose as your answer the one of the four names given which should be filed FIRST according to the usual system of alphabetical filing of names, as described in the following paragraph.

In filing names, you must start with the last name. Names are filed in order of the first letter of the last name, then the second letter, etc. Therefore, BAILY would be filed before BROWN, which would be filed before COLT. A name with fewer letters of the same type comes first, i.e., Smith before Smithe. If the last names are the same, the names are filed alphabetically by the first name. If the first name is an initial, a name with an initial would come before a first name that starts with the same letter as the initial. Therefore, I. BROWN would come before IRA BROWN. Finally, if both last name and first name are the same, the name would be filed alphabetically by the middle name, once again an initial coming before a middle name which starts with the same letter as the initial. If there is no middle name at all, the name would come before those with middle initials or names.

SAMPLE QUESTION:
A. Lester Daniels
B. William Dancer
C. Nathan Danzig
D. Dan Lester

The last names beginning with D are filed before the last name beginning with L. Since DANIELS, DANCER, and DANZIG all begin with the same three letters, you must look at the fourth letter of the last name to determine which name should be filed first. C comes before I or Z in the alphabet, so DANCER is filed before DANIELS or DANZIG. Therefore, the answer to the above sample question is B.

5. A. Scott Biala
    B. Mary Byala
    C. Martin Baylor
    D. Francis Bauer

5._____

6. A. Howard J. Black
    B. Howard Black
    C. J. Howard Black
    D. John H. Black

6._____

7. A. Theodora Garth Kingston
    B. Theadore Barth Kingston
    C. Thomas Kingston
    D. Thomas T. Kingston

7._____

8. A. Paulette Mary Huerta
   B. Paul M. Huerta
   C. Paulette L. Huerta
   D. Peter A. Huerta

8._____

9. A. Martha Hunt Morgan
   B. Martin Hunt Morgan
   C. Mary H. Morgan
   D. Martine H. Morgan

9._____

10. A. James T. Meerschaum
    B. James M. Mershum
    C. James F. Mearshaum
    D. James N. Meshum

10._____

Questions 11-14.

DIRECTIONS: Questions 11 through 14 are to be answered SOLELY on the basis of the following information.

You are required to file various documents in file drawers which are labeled according to the following pattern:

DOCUMENTS

MEMOS		LETTERS	
File	Subject	File	Subject
84PM1	(A-L)	84PC1	(A-L)
84PM2	(M-Z)	84PC2	(M-Z)

REPORTS		INQUIRIES	
File	Subject	File	Subject
84PR1	(A-L)	84PQ1	(A-L)
84PR2	(M-Z)	84PQ2	(M-Z)

11. A letter dealing with a burglary should be filed in the drawer labeled
    A. 84PM1 B. 84PC1 C. 84PR1 D. 84PQ2

11._____

12. A report on Statistics should be found in the drawer labeled
    A. 84PM1 B. 84PC2 C. 84PR2 D. 84PQS

12._____

13. An inquiry is received about parade permit procedures. It should be filed in the drawer labeled
    A. 84PM2 B. 84PC1 C. 84PR1 D. 84PQ2

13._____

14. A police officer has a question about a robbery report you filed. You should pull this file from the drawer labeled
    A. 84PM1 B. 84PM2 C. 84PR1 D. 84PR2

14._____

Questions 15-22.

DIRECTIONS: Each of Questions 15 through 22 consists of four or six numbered names. For each question, choose the option (A, B, C, or D) which indicates the order in which the names should be filed in accordance with the following filing instructions:
- File alphabetically according to last name, then first name, then middle initial.
- File according to each successive letter within a name.
- When comparing two names in which the letters in the longer name are identical to the corresponding letters in the shorter name, the shorter name is filed first.
- When the last names are the same, initials are always filed before names beginning with the same letter.

15. I. Ralph Robinson
    II. Alfred Ross
    III. Luis Robles
    IV. James Roberts

    The CORRECT filing sequence for the above names should be
    A. IV, II, I, III   B. I, IV, III, II   C. III, IV, I, II   D. IV, I, III, II

16. I. Irwin Goodwin
    II. Inez Gonzalez
    III. Irene Goodman
    IV. Ira S. Goodwin
    V. Ruth I. Goldstein
    VI. M.B. Goodman

    The CORRECT filing sequence for the above names should be
    A. V, II, I, IV, III, VI   B. V, II, VI, III, IV, I
    C. V, II, III, VI, IV, I   D. V, II, III, VI, I, IV

17. I. George Allan
    II. Gregory Allen
    III. Gary Allen
    IV. George Allen

    The CORRECT filing sequence for the above names should be
    A. IV, III, I, II   B. I, IV, II, III   C. III, IV, I, II   D. I, III, IV, II

5 (#1)

18. I. Simon Kauffman
    II. Leo Kaufman
    III. Robert Kaufmann
    IV. Paul Kauffmann

    The CORRECT filing sequence for the above names should be
    A. I, IV, II, III   B. II, IV, III, I   C. III, II, IV, I   D. I, II, III, IV

    18.____

19. I. Roberta Williams
    II. Robin Wilson
    III. Roberta Wilson
    IV. Robin Williams

    The CORRECT filing sequence for the above names should be
    A. III, II, IV, I   B. I, IV, III, II   C. I, II, III, IV   D. III, I, II, IV

    19.____

20. I. Lawrence Shultz
    II. Albert Schultz
    III. Theodore Schwartz
    IV. Thomas Schwarz
    V. Alvin Schultz
    VI. Leonard Shultz

    The CORRECT filing sequence for the above names should be
    A. II, V, III, IV, I, VI   B. IV, III, V, I, II, VI
    C. II, V, I, VI, III, IV   D. I, VI, II, V, III, IV

    20.____

21. I. McArdle
    II. Mayer
    III. Maletz
    IV. McNiff
    V. Meyer
    VI. MacMahon

    The CORRECT filing sequence for the above names should be
    A. I, IV, VI, III, II, V   B. II, I, IV, VI, III, V
    C. VI, III, II, I, IV, V   D. VI, III, II, V, I, IV

    21.____

22. I. Jack E. Johnson
    II. R.H. Jackson
    III. Bertha Jackson
    IV. J.T. Johnson
    V. Ann Johns
    VI. John Jacobs

    The CORRECT filing sequence for the above names should be
    A. II, III, VI, V, IV, I   B. III, II, VI, V, IV, I
    C. VI, II, III, I, V, IV   D. III, II, VI, IV, V, I

    22.____

Questions 23-30.

DIRECTIONS: The code table below shows 10 letters with matching numbers. For each question, there are three sets of letters. Each set of letters is followed by a set of numbers which may or may not match their correct letter according to the code table. For each question, check all three sets of letters and numbers and mark your answer:
    A. if no pairs are correctly matched
    B. if only one pair is correctly matched
    C. if only two pairs are correctly matched
    D. if all three pairs are correctly matched

CODE TABLE

T	M	V	D	S	P	R	G	B	H
1	2	3	4	5	6	7	8	9	0

SAMPLE QUESTION: TMVDSP – 123456
                                    RGBHTM – 789011
                                    DSPRGB – 256789

In the sample question above, the first set of numbers correctly match its set of letters. But the second and third pairs contain mistakes. In the second pair, M is correctly matched with number 1. According to the code table, letter M should be correctly matched with number 2. In the third pair, the letter D is incorrectly matched with number 2. According to the code table, letter D should be correctly matched with number 4. Since only one of the pairs is correctly matched, the answer to this sample question is B.

23.   RSBMRM – 759262
       GDSRVH – 845730
       VDBRTM - 349713

24.   TGVSDR – 183247
       SMHRDP – 520647
       TRMHSR – 172057

25.   DSPRGM – 456782
       MVDBHT – 234902
       HPMDBT - 062491

26.   BVPTRD – 936184
       GDPHMB – 807029
       GMRHMV - 827032

27.   MGVRSH – 283750
       TRDMBS – 174295
       SPRMGV - 567283

28. SGBSDM – 489542
    MGHPTM – 290612
    MPBMHT - 269301

    28.____

29. TDPBHM – 146902
    VPBMRS – 369275
    GDMBHM - 842902

    29.____

30. MVPTBV – 236194
    PDRTMB – 47128
    BGTMSM - 981232

    30.____

KEY (CORRECT ANSWERS)

1.	A	11.	B	21.	C
2.	C	12.	C	22.	B
3.	B	13.	D	23.	B
4.	D	14.	D	24.	B
5.	D	15.	D	25.	C
6.	B	16.	C	26.	A
7.	B	17.	D	27.	D
8.	B	18.	A	28.	A
9.	A	19.	B	29.	D
10.	C	20.	A	30.	A

TEST 2

DIRECTIONS: Each question or incomplete statement is followed by several suggested answers or completions. Select the one that BEST answers the question or completes the statement. *PRINT THE LETTER OF THE CORRECT ANSWER IN THE SPACE AT THE RIGHT.*

Questions 1-10.

DIRECTIONS: Questions 1 through 10 each consists of two columns, each containing four lines of names, numbers and/or addresses. For each question, compare the lines in Column I with the lines in Column II to see if they match exactly, and mark your answer A, B, C, or D, according to the following instructions:
    A. all four lines match exactly
    B. only three lines match exactly
    C. only two lines match exactly
    D. only one line matches exactly

<u>COLUMN I</u>   <u>COLUMN II</u>

1.   I.   Earl Hodgson   Earl Hodgson   1.____
     II.   1409870   1408970
     III. Shore Ave.   Schore Ave.
     IV. Macon Rd.   Macon Rd.

2.   I.   9671485   9671485   2.____
     II.   470 Astor Court   470 Astor Court
     III. Halprin, Phillip   Halperin, Phillip
     IV. Frank D. Poliseo   Frank D. Poliseo

3.   I.   Tandem Associates   Tandom Associates   3.____
     II.   144-17 Northern Blvd. 144-17 Northern Blvd.
     III. Alberta Forchi   Albert Forchi
     IV. Kings Park, NY 10751   Kings Point, NY 10751

4.   I.   Bertha C. McCormack Bertha C. McCormack   4.____
     II.   Clayton, MO   Clayton, MO
     III. 976-4242   976-4242
     IV. New City, NY 10951   New City, NY 10951

5.   I.   George C. Morill   George C. Morrill   5.____
     II.   Columbia, SC 29201   Columbia, SD 29201
     III. Louis Ingham   Louis Ingham
     IV. 3406 Forest Ave.   3406 Forest Ave.

6.   I.   506 S. Elliott Pl.   506 S. Elliott Pl.   6.____
     II.   Herbert Hall   Hurbert Hall
     III. 4712 Rockaway Pkway 4712 Rockaway Pkway
     IV. 169 E. 7 St.   169 E. 7 St.

7.
  I. 345 Park Ave.   345 Park Pl.   7.____
  II. Colman Oven Corp.   Coleman Oven Corp.
  III. Robert Conte   Robert Conti
  IV. 6179846   6179846

8.
  I. Grigori Schierber   Grigori Schierber   8.____
  II. Des Moines, Iowa   Des Moines, Iowa
  III. Gouverneur Hospital   Gouverneur Hospital
  IV. 91-35 Cresskill Pl.   91-35 Cresskill Pl.

9.
  I. Jeffery Janssen   Jeffrey Janssen   9.____
  II. 8041071   8041071
  III. 40 Rockefeller Plaza   40 Rockafeller Plaza
  IV. 407 6 St.   406 7 St.

10.
  I. 5971996   5871996   10.____
  II. 3113 Knickerbocker Ave. 31123 Knickerbocker Ave.
  III. 8434 Boston Post Rd.   8424 Boston Post Rd.
  IV. Penn Station   Penn Station

Questions 11-14.

DIRECTIONS: Questions 11 through 14 are to be answered by looking at the four groups of names and addresses listed below (I, II, III, and IV), and then finding out the number of groups that have their corresponding numbered lies exactly the same.

	GROUP I	GROUP II
Line 1.	Richmond General Hospital	Richman General Hospital
Line 2.	Geriatric Clinic	Geriatric Clinic
Line 3.	3975 Paerdegat St.	3975 Peardegat St.
Line 4.	Loudonville, New York 11538	Londonville, New York 11538

	GROUP III	GROUP IV
Line 1.	Richmond General Hospital	Richmend General Hospital
Line 2.	Geriatric Clinic	Geriatric Clinic
Line 3.	3795 Paerdegat St.	3975 Paerdegat St.
Line 4.	Loudonville, New York 11358	Loudonville, New York 11538

1. In how many groups is line one exactly the same?   11.____
   A. Two   B. Three   C. Four   D. None

12. In how many groups is line two exactly the same?   12.____
    A. Two   B. Three   C. Four   D. None

13. In how many groups is line three exactly the same?   13.____
    A. Two   B. Three   C. Four   D. None

14. In how many groups is line four exactly the same? 14.____
    A. Two   B. Three   C. Four   D. None

Questions 15-18.

DIRECTIONS: Each of Questions 15 through 18 has two lists of names and addresses. Each list contains three sets of names and addresses. Check each of the three sets in the list on the right to see if they are the same as the corresponding set in the list on the left. Mark your answers:
   A. if none of the sets in the right list are the same as those in the left list
   B. if only one of the sets in the right list is the same as those in the left list
   C. if only two of the sets in the right list are the same as those in the left list
   D. if all three sets in the right list are the same as those in the left list

15. Mary T. Berlinger   Mary T. Berlinger   15.____
    2351 Hampton St.   2351 Hampton St.
    Monsey, N.Y. 20117   Monsey, N.Y. 20117

    Eduardo Benes   Eduardo Benes
    483 Kingston Avenue   473 Kingston Avenue
    Central Islip, N.Y. 11734   Central Islip, N.Y. 11734

    Alan Carrington Fuchs   Alan Carrington Fuchs
    17 Gnarled Hollow Road   17 Gnarled Hollow Road
    Los Angeles, CA 91635   Los Angeles, CA 91685

16. David John Jacobson   David John Jacobson   16.____
    178 34 St. Apt. 4C   178 53 St. Apt. 4C
    New York, N.Y. 00927   New York, N.Y. 00927

    Ann-Marie Calonella   Ann-Marie Calonella
    7243 South Ridge Blvd.   7243 South Ridge Blvd.
    Bakersfield, CA 96714   Bakersfield, CA 96714

    Pauline M. Thompson   Pauline M. Thomson
    872 Linden Ave.   872 Linden Ave.
    Houston, Texas 70321   Houston, Texas 70321

17. Chester LeRoy Masterton   Chester LeRoy Masterson   17.____
    152 Lacy Rd.   152 Lacy Rd.
    Kankakee, Ill. 54532   Kankakee, Ill. 54532

    William Maloney   William Maloney
    S. LaCrosse Pla.   S. LaCross Pla.
    Wausau, Wisconsin 52136   Wausau, Wisconsin 52146

    Cynthia V. Barnes   Cynthia V. Barnes
    16 Pines Rd.   16 Pines Rd.
    Greenpoint, Miss. 20376   Greenpoint,, Miss. 20376

18. Marcel Jean Frontenac   Marcel Jean Frontenac   18.____
    8 Burton On The Water   6 Burton On The Water
    Calender, Me. 01471   Calender, Me. 01471

    J. Scott Marsden   J. Scott Marsden
    174 S. Tipton St.   174 Tipton St.
    Cleveland, Ohio   Cleveland, Ohio

    Lawrence T. Haney   Lawrence T. Haney
    171 McDonough St.   171 McDonough St.
    Decatur, Ga. 31304   Decatur, Ga. 31304

Questions 19-26.

DIRECTIONS: Each of Questions 19 through 26 has two lists of numbers. Each list contains three sets of numbers. Check each of the three sets in the list on the right to see if they are the same as the corresponding set in the list on the left. Mark your answers:
- A. if none of the sets in the right list are the same as those in the left list
- B. if only one of the sets in the right list is the same as those in the left list
- C. if only two of the sets in the right list are the same as those in the left list
- D. if all three sets in the right list are the same as those in the left lists

19. 7354183476   7354983476   19.____
    4474747744   4474747774
    5791430231   57914302311

20. 7143592185   7143892185   20.____
    8344517699   8344518699
    9178531263   9178531263

21. 2572114731   257214731   21.____
    8806835476   8806835476
    8255831246   8255831246

22. 331476853821   331476858621   22.____
    6976658532996   6976655832996
    3766042113715   3766042113745

23. 8806663315   88066633115   23.____
    74477138449   74477138449
    211756663666   211756663666

24. 990006966996   99000696996   24.____
     53022219743   53022219843
     4171171117717   4171171177717

25. 24400222433004   24400222433004   25.____
     5300030055000355   5300030055500355
     20000075532002022   20000075532002022

26. 6111666406600011116   61116664066001116   26.____
     7111300117001100733   7111300117001100733
     26666446664476518   26666446664476518

Questions 27-30.

DIRECTIONS: Questions 27 through 30 are to be answered by picking the answer which is in the correct numerical order, from the lowest number to the highest number, in each question.

27. A. 44533, 44518, 44516, 44547   27.____
     B. 44516, 44518, 44533, 44547
     C. 44547, 44533, 44518, 44516
     D. 44518, 44516, 44547, 44533

28. A. 95587, 95593, 95601, 95620   28.____
     B. 95601, 95620, 95587, 95593
     C. 95593, 95587, 95601. 95620
     D. 95620, 95601, 95593, 95587

29. A. 232212, 232208, 232232, 232223   29.____
     B. 232208, 232223, 232212, 232232
     C. 232208, 232212, 232223, 232232
     D. 232223, 232232, 232208, 232208

30. A. 113419, 113521, 113462, 113462   30.____
     B. 113588, 113462, 113521, 113419
     C. 113521, 113588, 113419, 113462
     D. 113419, 113462, 113521, 113588

KEY (CORRECT ANSWERS)

1.	C	11.	A	21.	C
2.	B	12.	C	22.	A
3.	D	13.	A	23.	D
4.	A	14.	A	24.	A
5.	C	15.	C	25.	C
6.	B	16.	B	26.	C
7.	D	17.	B	27.	B
8.	A	18.	B	28.	A
9.	D	19.	B	29.	C
10.	C	20.	B	30.	D

NAME AND NUMBER CHECKING
EXAMINATION SECTION
TEST 1

DIRECTIONS: This test is designed to measure your speed/and accuracy. You are urged to work both quickly and accurately and to do correctly as many lists as you can in the time allowed. The test consists of lists or pairs of names and numbers. Count the number of IDENTICAL pairs in each list. Then, select the correct number, 1, 2, 3, 4, 5, and indicate your choice in the space at the right. Two sample questions are presented for your guidance, together with the correct solutions.

<u>SAMPLE LIST A</u>
Adelphi College	– Adelphia College
Braxton Corp	– Braxeton Corp.
Wassaic State School	– Wassaic State School
Central Islip State Hospital	– Central Isllip State Hospital
Greenwich House	– Greenwich House

NOTE: There are only two correct pairs—Wassaic State School and Greenwich House. Therefore, the CORRECT answer is 2.

<u>SAMPLE LIST B</u>
78453694	– 78453684
784530	– 784530
533	– 534
67845	– 67845
2368745	– 2368755

NOTE: There are only two correct pairs—784530 and 67845. Therefore, the CORRECT answer is 2.

<u>LIST 1</u>   1.____
98654327	- 98654327
74932564	- 7492564
61438652	- 61438652
01297653	- 01287653
1865439765	- 1865439765

<u>LIST 2</u>   2.____
478362	- 478363
278354792	- 278354772
9327	- 9327
297384625	- 27384625
6428156	- 6428158

LIST 3
    Abbey House — - Abbey House
    Actor's Fund Home — - Actor's Fund Home
    Adrian Memorial — - Adrian Memorial
    A. Clayton Powell Home — - Clayton Powell House
    Abbot E. Kittredge Club — - Abbott E. Kitteredge Club

3.____

LIST 4
    3682 — - 3692
    21937453829 — - 31927453829
    723 — - 733
    2763920 — - 2763920
    47293 — - 47293

4.____

LIST 5
    Adra House — - Adra House
    Adolescents' Court — - Adolescents' Court
    Cliff Villa — - Cliff Villa
    Clark Neighborhood House — - Clark Neighborhood House
    Alma Mathews House — - Alma Mathews House

5.____

LIST 6
    28734291 — - 28734271
    63810263849 — - 63810263846
    26831027 — - 26831027
    368291 — - 368291
    7238102637 — - 7238102637

6.____

LIST 7
    Albion State T.S. — - Albion State T.C.
    Clara de Hirsch Home — - Clara De Hirsch Home
    Alice Carrington Royce — - Alice Carington Royce
    Alice Chopin Nursery — - Alice Chapin Nursery
    Lighthouse Eye Clinic — - Lighthouse Eye Clinic

7.____

LIST 8
    327 — - 329
    712438291026 — - 712438291026
    2753829142 — - 275382942
    826287 — - 826289
    26435162839 — - 26435162839

8.____

LIST 9
    Letchworth Village — - Letchworth Village
    A.A.A.E. Inc. — - A.A.A.E. Inc.
    Clear Pool Camp — - Clear Pool Camp
    A.M.M.L.A. Inc. — - A.M.M.L.A. Inc.
    J.G. Harbard — - J.G. Harbord

9.____

LIST 10
		10._____
8254	- 8256	
2641526	- 2641526	
4126389012	- 4126389102	
725	- 725	
76253917287	- 76253917287	

LIST 11
		11._____
Attica State Prison	- Attica State Prison	
Nellie Murrah	- Nellie Murrah	
Club Marshall	- Club Marshal	
Assissium Casea-Maria	- Assissium Casa-Maria	
The Homestead	- The Homestead	

LIST 12
		12._____
2691	- 2691	
623819253627	- 623819253629	
28637	- 28937	
278392736	- 278392736	
52739	- 52739	

LIST 13
		13._____
A.I.C.P. Boys Camp	- A.I.C.P. Boy's Camp	
Einar Chrystie	- Einar Christyie	
Astoria Center	- Astoria Center	
G. Frederick Brown	- G. Federick Browne	
Vacation Service	- Vacation Services	

LIST 14
		14._____
728352689	- 728352688	
643728	- 643728	
37829176	- 37827196	
8425367	- 8425369	
65382018	- 65382018	

LIST 15
		15._____
E.S. Streim	- E.S. Strim	
Charles E. Higgins	- Charles E. Higgins	
Baluvelt, N.Y.	- Blauwelt, N.Y.	
Roberta Magdalen	- Roberto Magdalen	
Ballard School	- Ballard School	

LIST 16
		16._____
7382	- 7392	
281374538299	- 291374538299	
623	- 633	
6273730	- 6273730	
63392	- 63392	

4 (#1)

LIST 17   17.____
    Orrin Otis — Orrin Otis
    Barat Settlement — Barat Settlemen
    Emmanuel House — Emmanuel House
    William T. McCreery — William T. McCreery
    Seamen's Home — Seaman's Home

LIST 18   18.____
    72824391 — 72834371
    3729106237 — 37291106237
    82620163849 — 82620163846
    37638921 — 37638921
    82631027 — 82631027

LIST 19   19.____
    Commonwealth Fund — Commonwealth Fund
    Anne Johnsen — Anne Johnson
    Bide-A-Wee Home — Bide-a-Wee Home
    Riverdale-on-Hudson — Riverdal-on-Hudson
    Bialystoker Home — Bailystoker Home

LIST 20   20.____
    9271 — 9271
    392918352627 — 392018852629
    72637 — 72637
    927392736 — 927392736
    92739 — 92739

LIST 21   21.____
    Charles M. Stump — Charles M. Stump
    Bourne Workshop — Buorne Workshop
    B'nai Bi'rith — B'nai Brith
    Poppenhuesen Institute — Poppenheusen Institute
    Consular Service — Consular Service

LIST 22   22.____
    927352689 — 927352688
    647382 — 648382
    93729176 — 93727196
    649536718 — 649536718
    5835367 — 5835369

LIST 23   23.____
    L.S. Bestend — L.S. Bestent
    Hirsch Mfg. Co. — Hircsh Mfg. Co.
    F.H. Storrs — F.P. Storrs
    Camp Wassaic — Camp Wassaic
    George Ballingham — George Ballingham

5 (#1)

LIST 24   24.____
    372846392048   - 372846392048
    334   - 334
    7283524678   - 7283524678
    7283   - 7283
    7283629372   - 7283629372

LIST 25   25.____
    Dr. Stiles Company   - Dr. Stills Company
    Frances Hunsdon   - Frances Hunsdon
    Northrop Barrert   - Nothrup Barrent
    J.D. Brunjes   - J.D. Brunjes
    Theo. Claudel & Co.   - Theo. Claudel co.

KEY (CORRECT ANSWERS)

1.	3		11.	3
2.	1		12.	3
3.	2		13.	1
4.	2		14.	2
5.	5		15.	2
6.	3		16.	2
7.	1		17.	3
8.	2		18.	2
9.	4		19.	2
10.	3		20.	4

21. 2
22. 1
23. 2
24. 5
25. 2

TEST 2

DIRECTIONS: This test is designed to measure your speed/and accuracy. You are urged to work both quickly and accurately and to do correctly as many lists as you can in the time allowed. The test consists of lists or pairs of names and numbers. Count the number of IDENTICAL pairs in each list. Then, select the correct number, 1, 2, 3, 4, 5, and indicate your choice in the space at the right.

LIST 1
    82728   - 82738
    82736292637   - 82736292639
    728   - 738
    83926192527   - 83726192529
    82736272   - 82736272

1.____

LIST 2
    L. Pietri   - L. Pietri
    Mathewson, L.F.   - Mathewson, L.F.
    Funk & Wagnall   - Funk & Wagnalls
    Shimizu, Sojio   - Shimizu, Sojio
    Filing Equipment Bureau - Filing Equipment Buraeu

2.____

LIST 3
    63801829374   - 63801839474
    283577657   - 283577657
    65689   - 65689
    3457892026   - 3547893026
    2779   - 2778

3.____

LIST 4
    August Caille   - August Caille
    The Well-Fare Service - The Wel-Fare Service
    K.L.M. Process co.   - R.L.M. Process Co.
    Merrill Littell   - Merrill Littell
    Dodd & Sons   - Dodd & Son

4.____

LIST 5
    998745732   - 998745733
    723   - 723
    463849102983   - 463849102983
    8570   - 8570
    279012   - 279012

5.____

LIST 6
    M.A. Wender   - M.A. Winder
    Minneapolis Supply Co. - Minneapolis Supply Co.
    Beverly Hills Corp   - Beverley Hills Corp.
    Trafalgar Square   - Trafalgar Square
    Phifer, D.T.   - Phiefer, D.T.

6.____

LIST 7
7834629	- 7834629
3549806746	- 3549806746
97802564	- 97892564
689246	- 688246
2578024683	- 2578024683

7.____

LIST 8
Scadrons'	- Scadrons'
Gensen & Bro.	- Genson & Bro.
Firestone Co.	- Firestone Co.
H.L. Eklund	- H.L. Eklund
Oleomargarine Co.	- Oleomargarine Co.

8.____

LIST 9
782039485618	- 782039485618
53829172639	- 63829172639
892	- 892
82937482	- 829374820
52937456	- 53937456

9.____

LIST 10
First Nat'l Bank	- First Nat'l Bank
Sedgwick Machine Works	- Sedgewick Machine Works
Hectographia Co.	- Hectographia Corp.
Levet Bros.	- Levet Bros.
Multistamp Co., Inc.	- Multistamp Co., Inc.

10.____

LIST 11
7293	- 7293
6382910293	- 6382910292
981928374012	- 981928374912
58293	- 58393
18203649271	- 283019283745

11.____

LIST 12
Lowrey Lb'r Co.	- Lowrey Lb'r Co.
Fidelity Service	- Fidelity Service
Reumann, J.A.	- Reumann, J.A.
Duophoto Ltd.	- Duophotos Ltd.
John Jarratt	- John Jaratt

12.____

LIST 13
6820384	- 6820384
383019283745	- 383019283745
63927102	- 63928102
91029354829	- 91029354829
58291728	- 58291728

13.____

LIST 14
- Standard Press Co.   - Standard Press Co.
- Reliant Mf'g. Co.   - Relant Mf'g Co.
- M.C. Lynn   - M.C. Lynn
- J. Fredericks Company   - G. Fredericks Company
- Wandermann, B.S.   - Wanderman, B.S.

14.____

LIST 15
- 4283910293   - 4283010203
- 992018273648   - 992018273848
- 620   - 629
- 752937273   - 752937373
- 5392   - 5392

15.____

LIST 16
- Waldorf Hotel   - Waldorf Hotel
- Aaron Machinery Co.   - Aaron Machinery Co.
- Caroline Ann Locke   - Caroline Ane Locke
- McCabe Mfg. Co.   - McCabe Mfg. Co.
- R.L. Landres   - R.L. Landers

16.____

LIST 17
- 68391028364   - 68391028394
- 68293   - 68293
- 739201   - 739201
- 72839201   - 72839211
- 739917   - 739719

17.____

LIST 18
- Balsam M.M.   - Balsamm, M.M.
- Steinway & Co.   - Stienway & M. Co.
- Eugene Elliott   - Eugene A. Elliott
- Leonard Loan Co.   - Leonard Loan Co.
- Frederick Morgan   - Frederick Morgen

18.____

LIST 19
- 8929   - 9820
- 392836472829   - 392836572829
- 462   - 4622039271
- 827   - 2039276837
- 53829   - 54829

19.____

LIST 20
- Danielson's Hofbrau   - Danielson's Hafbrau
- Edward A. Truarme   - Edward A. Truame
- Insulite Co.   - Insulite Co.
- Reisler Shoe Corp.   - Rielser Shoe Corp.
- L.L. Thompson   - L.L. Thompson

20.____

LIST 21
    92839102837   - 92839102837
    58891028   - 58891028
    7291728   - 7291928
    272839102839   - 272839102839
    428192   - 428102

21._____

LIST 22
    K.L. Veiller   - K.L. Veiller
    Webster, Roy   - Webster, Ray
    Drasner Spring Co.   - Drasner Spring Co.
    Edward J. Cravenport   - Edward J. Cravanport
    Harold Field   - Harold A. Field

22._____

LIST 23
    2293   - 2293
    4283910293   - 5382910292
    871928374012   - 871928374912
    68293   - 68393
    8120364927   - 81293649271

23._____

LIST 24
    Tappe, Inc   - Tappe, Inc.
    A.M. Wentingworth   - A.M. Wentinworth
    Scott A. Elliott   - Scott A. Elliott
    Echeverria Corp.   - Echeverria Corp.
    Bradford Victor Company   - Bradford Victer Company

24._____

LIST 25
    4820384   - 4820384
    393019283745   - 283919283745
    63917102   - 63927102
    91029354829   - 91029354829
    48291728   - 48291728

25._____

KEY (CORRECT ANSWERS)

1.	1	11.	1
2.	3	12.	3
3.	2	13.	4
4.	2	14.	2
5.	4	15.	1
6.	2	16.	3
7.	3	17.	2
8.	4	18.	1
9.	2	19.	1
10.	3	20.	2

21. 3
22. 2
23. 1
24. 2
25. 4

ARITHMETICAL REASONING
EXAMINATION SECTION
TEST 1

DIRECTIONS: Each question or incomplete statement is followed by several suggested answers or completions. Select the one that BEST answers the question or completes the statement. *PRINT THE LETTER OF THE CORRECT ANSWER IN THE SPACE AT THE RIGHT.*

1. Liquid toilet soap is supplied in 5-gallon cans. If each of the twelve toilet rooms in your building uses an average of one quart of toilet soap per month, the amount of cans you should be required to requisite to cover needs for a three month period is

   A. two   B. three   C. four   D. five

   1.____

2. A corridor is ten feet wide and 210 feet long. If it takes a two-man crew about one hour to mop 5,000 square feet, the amount of time required for mopping the corridor is MOST NEARLY _____ minutes.

   A. 30   B. 25
   C. 15   D. 10

   2.____

3. If 75 crates of food were ordered and 100 crates were delivered, then the shipment is larger than the number ordered by _____ crates.

   A. 10   B. 15   C. 25   D. 35

   3.____

4. If 200 boxes of merchandise were ordered and 100 boxes are delivered, then the shipment is short by _____ boxes.

   A. 50   B. 100   C. 150   D. 175

   4.____

5. You are to load a hand truck with cartons weighing a total of 200 pounds. If each carton weighs 20 pounds, then the TOTAL number of cartons to be loaded is

   A. 8   B. 9   C. 10   D. 11

   5.____

6. You are to unpack twelve cartons of paper and place the paper on a storage shelf. If each carton has eight packs of paper, then the number of packs of paper that you will place on the shelf is

   A. 72   B. 84   C. 96   D. 108

   6.____

7. If floor wax costs $2.90 a gallon, then the TOTAL cost of a carton in which there are six gallons of wax is

   A. $17.40   B. $19.00   C. $21.40   D. $29.00

   7.____

8. You know that a storage shelf unit can safely hold items up to a total weight of 300 pounds.
   If there are already 8 boxes of canned food on the shelves of the unit, all exactly the same, and each box weighs 25 pounds, then the number of the same boxes of canned food that you can safely add to those on the shelves is

   A. 4   B. 5   C. 6   D. 7

   8.____

9. During the month of June, 40,587 people attended a city-owned swimming pool. In July, 13,014 more people attended the swimming pool than the number that had attended in June. In August, 39,655 people attended the swimming pool. The TOTAL number of people who attended the swimming pool during the months of June, July, and August was

   A. 80,242   B. 93,256   C. 133,843   D. 210,382

10. Assume that your agency has been given $2,025 to purchase file cabinets.
    If each file cabinet costs $135, how many file cabinets can your agency purchase?

    A. 8   B. 10   C. 15   D. 16

11. Assume that your unit ordered 14 staplers at a total cost of $30.20, and each stapler cost the same.
    The cost of one stapler was MOST NEARLY

    A. $1.02   B. $1.61   C. $2.16   D. $2.26

12. Assume that you are responsible for counting and recording licensing fees collected by your department. On a particular day, your department collected in fees 40 checks in the amount of $6 each, 80 checks in the amount of $4 each, 45 twenty dollar bills, 30 ten dollar bills, 42 five dollar bills, and 186 one dollar bills.
    The TOTAL amount in fees collected on that day was

    A. $1,406   B. $1,706   C. $2,156   D. $2,356

13. Assume that you are responsible for your agency's petty cash fund. During the month of February, you pay out 7 subway fares at 50? each and one taxi fare for $2.85. You pay out nothing else from the fund. At the end of February, you count the money left in the fund and find 3 one dollar bills, 4 quarters, 5 dimes, and 4 nickels. The amount of money you had available in the petty cash fund at the BEGINNING of February was

    A. $4.70   B. $6.35   C. $7.55   D. $11.05

14. Assume that you are assigned to sell tickets at a city-owned ice skating rink. An adult ticket costs $1.50, and a children's ticket costs $.75. At the end of a day, you find that you have sold 36 adult tickets and 80 children's tickets.
    The TOTAL amount of money you collected for that day was

    A. $81.60   B. $106.00   C. $114.00   D. $116.00

15. If each office worker files 487 index cards in one hour, how many cards can 26 office workers file in one hour?

    A. 10,662   B. 12,175   C. 12,662   D. 14,266

16. Assume a city agency has 775 office workers.
    If 2 out of 25 office workers were absent on a particular day, how many office workers reported to work on that day?

    A. 713   B. 744   C. 750   D. 773

17. If a worker earns $9.18 per hour and works a 40-hour week, his weekly pay will be

    A. $357.20   B. $366.20   C. $366.40   D. $367.20

18. If a stock clerk earns $13.12 per hour and works a 40-hour week, how much will she receive in two weeks?

    A. $1,049.60   B. $1,049.80
    C. $1,050.60   D. $1,051.60

19. A stock clerk earns $9.18 per hour when he works a 40-hour week and is paid for overtime at time and a half for all time worked over 40 hours.
    How much money for overtime should he receive if he worked a 48-hour week?

    A. $109.16   B. $109.28   C. $110.16   D. $110.36

20. The reorder quantity is reached by multiplying the average monthly usage by the lead time (in months) and adding the minimum balance. For a particular item, the lead time is 2 months, the minimum balance is 100, and the average monthly usage is 150.
    The reorder quantity for this item is

    A. 300   B. 400   C. 600   D. 1,000

21. If a job can be completed by 4 employees in 6 days, how many days will it take 6 employees working at an equal speed to do the same job?

    A. 2   B. 3   C. 3 1/2   D. 4

22. If your rate of pay is $8.00 an hour for a 40-hour work week, and in an emergency you volunteer to work your half-hour lunch period for 5 days at straight time, what will your TOTAL gross pay be at the end of the week?

    A. $340   B. $350   C. $370   D. $380

23. If the gross weight of a trailer truck with a load of ferrous scrap removed from your storage yard is 67,130 pounds and the tare weight is 24,570 pounds, what is the weight, in gross tons, of the scrap removed?

    A. 17   B. 18   C. 19   D. 21

24. You receive a requisition for 2 1/2 gross of machine screws. The number of machine screws you should dispense is

    A. 300   B. 324   C. 360   D. 400

25. A requisition for a ream of paper is a request for how many sheets of paper?

    A. 200   B. 500   C. 750   D. 1,000

KEY (CORRECT ANSWERS)

1. A
2. B
3. C
4. B
5. C

6. C
7. A
8. A
9. C
10. C

11. C
12. C
13. D
14. C
15. C

16. A
17. D
18. A
19. C
20. B

21. D
22. A
23. D
24. C
25. B

SOLUTIONS TO PROBLEMS

1. (12)(1 qt.) = 12 qts. = 3 gallons per month. For 3 months, 9 gallons are needed. Since the soap is supplied in 5-gallon cans, 2 cans are required.

2. (10')(210') = 2100 sq.ft. Time required = (2100/5000) hrs. = .42 hrs. - 25 min. (Closest answer given is 30 min.)

3. 100 - 75 = 25 crates

4. 200 - 100 = 100 boxes

5. 200 20 = 10 cartons

6. (12) (8) = 96 packs of paper

7. ($2.90)(6) = $17.40

8. Maximum allowable number of boxes = 300 ÷ 25 = 12. Since there are already 8 boxes on the shelves, 4 more may be added.

9. Total number of people = 40,587 + 53,601 + 39,655 = 133,843

10. $2025 $135 = 15 file cabinets

11. $30.20 14 = $2.16 per stapler

12. (40)($6) + (80)($4) + (45)($20) + (30)($10) + (42)($5) + (186)($1) = $2156

13. (7)($.50) + (1)($2.85) + (3)($1) + (4)($.25) + (5)($.10) + (4)($.05) = $11.05

14. (36)($1.50) + (80)($.75) = $114.00

15. (26)(487) = 12,662 cards

16. 16. Since 23 out of 25 were present, this represents .92 of these workers. Then, (.92)(775) = 713

17. ($9.18)(40) = $367.20

18. ($13.12)(40)(2) = $1049.60

19. ($9.18)(40) + ($13.77)(8) = $477.36 total, but his overtime is (13.77)(8) = $110.16

20. Reorder quantity = (150)(2) + 100 = 400

21. (4)(6) = 24 employee-days. Then, 24 ÷ 6 = 4 days

22. ($8.00)(40) + ($8.00)(2.5) = $340

6 (#1)

23. 67,130 - 24,570 = 42,560 lbs. 2,000 = 21.28 tons = 21 tons

24. (2 1/2)(144) = 360 machine screws

25. 1 ream = 500 sheets of paper

TEST 2

DIRECTIONS: Each question or incomplete statement is followed by several suggested answers or completions. Select the one that BEST answers the question or completes the statement. *PRINT THE LETTER OF THE CORRECT ANSWER IN THE SPACE AT THE RIGHT.*

1. A bin in your storeroom measuring 2' x 1.5' x 4' has a storage volume of _____ cubic feet.   1._____

   A. 12 B. 24 C. 50 D. 72

2. A gill is equivalent to 8 fluid ounces.   2._____
   How many gills are required to fill a 5-gallon container with distilled water?

   A. 70 B. 75 C. 80 D. 85

3. A storage space 8'6" wide and 9'6" long has an area that is CLOSEST to _____ square feet.   3._____

   A. 80 B. 81 C. 82 D. 83

4. A drill bit has a diameter of 13/32 inch.   4._____
   Of the following, the decimal number CLOSEST to 13/32 is

   A. 0.406 B. 0.408 C. 0.410 D. 0.412

5. If repaired units come into your storeroom in a palletized container indicating that the gross weight is 2250 pounds, then the   5._____

   A. container alone weighs 2250 pounds
   B. repaired units alone weigh 2250 pounds
   C. repaired units and palletized container weigh 2250 pounds
   D. weight of 2250 pounds is approximate

6. You have 5 pieces of lumber. Their lengths are: 8'2", 6'4", 3'4", 5'9", and 4'5".   6._____
   What is the sum of the lengths of the 5 pieces of lumber?

   A. 26' B. 26'9" C. 27'10" D. 28'

7. A full reel of 1,000 feet of power distribution cable weighs 8,095 pounds. The cable weighs 7.6 pounds per foot. The weight of the empty reel is _____ pounds.   7._____

   A. 465 B. 480 C. 495 D. 510

8. A crate 2' by 3' by 6' has a volume of _____ cubic yards.   8._____

   A. 6 B. 1 1/3 C. 18 D. 4

9. Of 600 pieces received in a shipment, 50 are inspected. Of the 50, 10 are found damaged.   9._____
   If the 50 are a representative sampling, the number of items in the entire shipment LIKELY to be damaged is

   A. 50 B. 60 C. 80 D. 120

10. A board having 3 square feet has how many square inches? 10.____
    A. 144 B. 288 C. 432 D. 576

11. A crate of material delivered to your storeroom has inscribed on it the words *Net Weight 250 pounds.* 11.____
    This means that the

    A. weight of 250 pounds is approximate
    B. material and crate together weigh 250 pounds
    C. material alone weighs 250 pounds
    D. crate alone weighs 250 pounds

12. A box contains an equal number of brass and copper tubes. Each brass tube weighs 4 pounds, each copper tube weighs 1 pound, and the empty box weighs 5 pounds. The total weight of the box and tubes is 200 pounds. 12.____
    The TOTAL number of tubes in the box is

    A. 39 B. 60 C. 78 D. 156

13. A caretaker received $70.00 for having worked from Monday through Friday, 9 M. to 5 P.M., with one hour a day for lunch. 13.____
    The number of hours the caretaker would have to work to earn $12.00 is

    A. 10   B. 6
    C. 70 divided by 12 D. 70 minus 12

14. If the cost of a broom went up from $4.00 to $6.00, the percent INCREASE in the original cost is 14.____
    A. 20 B. 25 C. 33 1/3 D. 50

15. The AVERAGE of the numbers 3, 5, 7, 8, 12 is 15.____
    A. 5 B. 6 C. 7 D. 8

16. The cost of 100 bags of cotton cleaning cloths, 89 pounds per bag, at 7 cents per pound, is 16.____
    A. $549.35 B. $623.00 C. $700.00 D. $890.00

17. If 5 1/2 bags of sweeping compound cost $55.00, then 6 1/2 bags would cost 17.____
    A. $60.00 B. $62.50 C. $65.00 D. $67.00

18. The cost of cleaning supplies in a project averaged $330.00 a month during the first 8 months of the year. How much can be spent each month for the last four months if the total amount that can be spent for cleaning supplies for the year is $3,880? 18.____
    A. $124.00 B. $220.00 C. $310.00 D. $330.00

19. A shelf in a supply closet can safely hold only 100 pounds. A package of paper towels weighs 2 pounds, a carton of disinfectant weighs 8 pounds, and a box of soap weighs 1 pound. There are already 6 cartons of disinfectant and 6 boxes of soap on the shelf. How many packages of towels can be SAFELY placed there? 19.____
    A. 20 B. 23 C. 25 D. 27

20. A cleaning solution is made up of 4 gallons of water, 1 pint of liquid soap, and 1 pint of ammonia.
    How many gallons of water are needed to use up a gallon of ammonia? 20._____
    A. 8   B. 16   C. 24   D. 32

21. Suppose a caretaker has 50 stair halls to clean. If he cleans 74% of them, the number of stair halls still UNCLEANED is 21._____
    A. 38   B. 26   C. 24   D. 13

22. If a man has a 12 foot piece of wood and wishes to cut it into two pieces so that one piece is twice as long as the other, the LONGER piece should be _____ feet. 22._____
    A. 7   B. 7 1/2   C. 8   D. 8 1/2

23. If fuel oil costs $1.09 9/10 per gallon, and $224 was the total cost for a tank fill-up, how many gallons were delivered? 23._____
    A. 203.82   B. 190.59   C. 217.38   D. 179.97

24. A drill bit has a diameter of 17/36". Of the following, the decimal equivalent CLOSEST to 17/36 is 24._____
    A. 0.444   B. 0.531   C. 0.473   D. 0.472

25. If cleaning solution costs $1.53 per gallon, what is the TOTAL cost of 2 cartons of cleaning solution when each carton holds 12 one-gallon jugs? 25._____
    A. $36.24   B. $36.72   C. $39.12   D. $37.92

KEY (CORRECT ANSWERS)

1. A
2. C
3. B
4. A
5. C

6. D
7. C
8. B
9. D
10. C

11. C
12. C
13. B
14. D
15. C

16. B
17. C
18. C
19. B
20. D

21. D
22. C
23. A
24. D
25. B

———

SOLUTIONS TO PROBLEMS

1. Volume = (21)(1.5')(4') = 12 cu.ft.

2. 5 gallons = (128)(5) = 640 fluid oz. Then, 640 8 = 80 gills

3. Area = (8'6")(9'6") = (8.5')(9.5') = 80.75 = 81 sq.ft.

4. 13/32 = .40625 = .406

5. Gross weight = combined weight of repaired units and palletized container.

6. 8'2" + 6'4" + 3'4" + 5'9" + 4'5" = 26'24" = 28'

7. Empty reel weight = 8095 - (7.6)(1000) = 495 lbs.

8. (2')(3')(6') = 36 cu.ft. = 36/27 = 1 1/2 cu.yds.

9. 10/50 = 20%. Then, (20%)(600) = 120 are likely to be damaged.

10. 3 sq.ft. = (3)(144) = 432 sq.in.

11. Net weight refers to the contents of the crate, not including the crate's weight.

12. Let x = number of brass and copper tubes together. Then, $(1/2x)(4) + (1/2)(1) + 5 = 200$. Simplifying, we get $2.5x = 195$. Solving, $x = 78$

13. $70 is paid for (7)(5) = 35 hrs., which means $2 per hour. Thus, $12 is received in 12/2 = 6 hours.

14. Percent increase = ($2.00/$4.00)(100) = 50%

15. Average = (3+5+7+8+12)/5 = 35/5 = 7

16. Cost = (100)(89)($.07) = $623.00

17. $55 ÷ 5.5 = $10 per bag. Then, 6 1/2 bags cost (6 1/2)($10) = $65.00

18. Let x = amount spent during each of the last 4 months. Then, $(8)($330) + 4x = 3880. Solving, $x = 310.00

19. Let x = number of pkgs. of towels. Then, $2x + (6)(8) + (6)(1) = 100$. Simplifying, $2x = 46$. Solving, $x = 23$

20. Since 1 gallon = 8 pints, 1 gallon of ammonia requires (4)(8) = 32 gallons of water

21. Number of stair halls uncleaned = (.26)(50) = 13

22. Let x = longer piece, $1/2x$ = shorter piece. Then, $x + 1/2x = 12$. Solving, $x = 8$ ft.

23. $224 ÷ $1.099 ≈ 203.82 gallons

24. $17/36 = .47\overline{2} \approx .472$

25. Total cost = (2)(12)($1.53) = $36.72

TEST 3

DIRECTIONS: Each question or Incomplete statement is followed by several suggested answers or completions. Select the one that BEST answers the question or completes the statement. *PRINT THE LETTER OF THE CORRECT ANSWER IN THE SPACE AT THE RIGHT.*

1. A storeroom is 100 feet long and 26 feet wide. One aisle 8 feet wide runs the length of the storeroom.
   One aisle 4 feet wide runs the width of the storeroom. If there were no other aisles, the number of square feet of usable storage space would be

   A. 1696 B. 1728 C. 2280 D. 2568   1.____

2. A discount of 1% is given on all purchases of a certain item In quantities of 100 units or more. An additional discount of 1% is given on that portion of the purchase which exceeds 300.
   If 450 units are purchased at a list price of $6.00, the total cost is

   A. $2,619 B. $2,664 C. $2,670 D. $2,682   2.____

3. The number of cartons measuring 3'x3'x2' which will be needed to pack 1,728 boxed Items each measuring 3"x9"x6" is

   A. 9 B. 18 C. 108 D. 192   3.____

4. A space 5 1/2 feet wide and 2 1/3 feet long has an area measured MOST NEARLY _____ square feet.

   A. 9 B. 10 C. 11 D. 12   4.____

5. One man is able to load two 2 1/2 ton trucks In one hour. To load ten such trucks, it will take ten men hour(s).

   A. 1/2 B. 1 C. 2 D. 2 1/2   5.____

6. If the average height of the stacks In your section of the storehouse is 10', the area which will be occupied by 56,000 cubic feet of supplies, is MOST LIKELY to be

   A. 70'x80' B. 60'x90' C. 50'x60' D. 560'x100'   6.____

7. The number of cartons, each measuring two cubic feet, which can fit into a space which is 100 square feet in area and Is 8' high is

   A. 50 B. 200 C. 400 D. 800   7.____

8. When the floor area measures 200' by 200' and the maximum weight it can hold is 4,000 tons, then the safe floor load is _____ pounds per square foot.

   A. 20 B. 160 C. 200 D. 400   8.____

9. A carton 1' x 1' x 3' measures _____ cubic yard(s).

   A. 1/3 B. 1/9 C. 3 D. 9   9.____

10. You have received 6 cartons, each containing 60 boxes of staples, priced at $36.00 per carton.
    The price per box is

    A. $.10   B. $.60   C. $3.60   D. $6.00

11. The amount of space in cubic feet, required to store 100 boxes each, measuring 24" x 12" x 6", is

    A. 10   B. 100   C. 168   D. 1,008

12. Assume that it takes an average of 2 man-hours to stack 1 ton of certain supplies. In order to stack 30 tons, the number of men required to complete the job in ten hours is

    A. 6   B. 10   C. 15   D. 30

13. An area measures 20'x22 1/2'. The floor load is 100 lbs. per square foot.
    The total weight that can be stored in this area is MOST NEARLY _____ lbs.

    A. 450   B. 9,000   C. 22,500   D. 45,000

14. The price of a certain type of linoleum is $1.00 per square foot.
    The total cost of four pieces of 9'x12' linoleum is MOST NEARLY

    A. $105   B. $400   C. $430   D. $2,160

15. The number of board feet in a piece of lumber measuring 2" thick by 2' wide by 12' long is

    A. 12   B. 16   C. 24   D. 48

KEY (CORRECT ANSWERS)

1. B	6. A	11. B
2. B	7. C	12. A
3. A	8. C	13. D
4. D	9. B	14. C
5. A	10. B	15. D

SOLUTIONS TO PROBLEMS

1. (26-8)(100-4) = 1728 sq.ft. of usable space

2. 300 1% @ $5.94 = $1782; 150 2% @ $5.88 = $882. $1782 + $882 = $2664

3. (3' 3')(3' 9")(2' 6") = (12)(4)(4) = 192 boxes per carton Then, 1728 192 = 9 cartons

4. (5 1/4')(2 1/3') = 12 1/4 sq.ft. = 12 sq.ft.

5. One man could load 10 trucks in 5 hrs. Thus, 10 men would need 5/10 = 1/2 hr. to load these 10 trucks.

6. 56,000 ÷ 10' = 5600 sq.ft. Selection A which is 70'x80' would yield 5600 sq.ft.

7. (100)(8) = 800 cu.ft., and 800 2 = 400

8. (200')(200') = 40,000 sq.ft. Then, (4000)(2000) 40,000 = 200 lbs. per sq.ft.

9. (1')(1')(3') = 3 cu.ft. = 3/27 = 1/9 cu.yd.

10. $36.00 60 = $.60 per box

11. (100)(2')(1')(1/2') = 100 cu.ft.

12. 30 tons requires (2) (30) = 60 man-hours. Then, 60 10 = 6 men.

13. (100)(20')(22 1/2) = 45,000 lbs.

14. ($1.00)(9')(12')(4) = $432 = $430

15. Each side of board = (2')(12') = 24 sq.ft. Total area = (2) (24) = 48 sq.ft.

www.ingramcontent.com/pod-product-compliance
Lightning Source LLC
Chambersburg PA
CBHW082210300426
44117CB00016B/2744